PENGUIN BOOKS

THE PENGUIN BOOK OF CHILDHOOD

Michael Rosen has been described as the 'poet laureate of postwar youth'. He has over a hundred books for children to his name, nearly all of which are a wicked mix of rumbustious humour, wordplay and sharp observation. He is a regular contributor to radio and TV, hosting BBC Radio 4's *Treasure Islands* and BBC World Service's *Meridian Books*. His research into children's literature and children's own writing takes him all over the world – the USA, Canada and Australia – and in the last twenty years he has visited over a thousand schools to perform his work. He has written several books for adults, including *Goodies and Daddies*, a light-hearted guide to fatherhood, and has co-edited *The Chatto Book of Dissent*. He is currently researching the changing portrayal of childhood in children's literature.

THE PENGUIN BOOK OF

CHILDHOOD

MICHAEL ROSEN

PENGUIN BOOKS

PENGUIN BOOKS

Published by the Penguin Group
Penguin Books Ltd, 27 Wrights Lane, London W8 5TZ, England
Penguin Books USA Inc., 375 Hudson Street, New York, New York 10014, USA
Penguin Books Australia Ltd, Ringwood, Victoria, Australia
Penguin Books Canada Ltd, 10 Alcorn Avenue, Toronto, Ontario, Canada M4V 3B2
Penguin Books (NZ) Ltd, 182–190 Wairau Road, Auckland 10, New Zealand

Penguin Books Ltd, Registered Offices: Harmondsworth, Middlesex, England

First published by Viking 1994
Published in Penguin Books 1995
1 3 5 7 9 10 8 6 4 2

Printed in England by Clays Ltd, St Ives plc

Contents

Introduction   1

Dad knows best: Ancient Egypt (New Kingdom), 2000–1500 BC   3

Pupil to teacher: Ancient Egypt (New Kingdom), 2000–1500 BC   3

Grave message: Inscription on the tomb of Thothrekh, Ancient
Egypt, Late Period (1000 BC–AD 100)   3

What to do with boys: Protagoras (*c.* 485–*c.* 415 BC), Ancient
Greece   4

Girls play 'The Tortoise': A game of Ancient Greece   5

Iphis speaks: Euripides (480–406 BC), from *Suppliant Women*,
Ancient Greece   5

Creon speaks: Sophocles (496–406 BC), Ancient Greece   6

Decline in standards: Socrates (469–399 BC)   6

Bedwetting explained: Lucretius, from *De Rerum Natura*, *c.* 80 BC   6

A brave girl: Pliny (*c.* AD 23–79), on the death of a girl,
Ancient Rome   7

The beastly foreigners: Plutarch on the Carthaginians, writing
c. AD 50   7

Castration not complex: Paulus Aegineta, Ancient Rome   8

Romans on childhood: Marcus Aurelius (AD 121–80) ; Seneca
(*c.* 4 BC–AD 65); Cicero (106–43 BC)   8

Mutilating children for freak shows: Seneca, writing *c.* AD 50   9

Vipstanus Messalla complains: Tacitus in *Dialogus de Oratoribus*,
c. AD 100   9

Ducks and drakes: Minucius Felix, near Rome, *c.* AD 300   10

Dear Dad . . .: Letter written in Greece, *c.* AD 300   10

Naughty: From St Augustine's *Confessions*, *c.* AD 364   11

Granddad's words of wisdom: Ausonius, Gallic professor of
rhetoric, to his six-year-old grandson, 4th century   11

Boy-kings are a pain: Historian, Rome, *c.* AD 500   12

At the school for monks: Aelfric, *Colloquy*, Cerne Abbas,
England, *c.* AD 900   12

In the sand-pit: From the autobiography of Gerald of Wales,
c. 1155   14

Fear of candles: William of Malmesbury writing in the 12th
century about Ethelred the Unready (born *c.* 969)   14

Are they not human?: Eadmer, England, *c.* 1100   15

She loves me, she loves me not . . .: Walther von der
Vogelweider, Holland or Germany, *c.* 1200   17

Equality some way off: Paulo of Certaldo, Middle Ages   17

Justice: Philip of Beaumanoir, end of 13th century   17

Body contact in the monastery: Custumal of Bec, Middle Ages   18

Medieval romping: Cuvelier, France, Middle Ages   18

A bit young for the job: From *Exempla*, stories for the use of
preachers, by Jacques de Vitry, Paris, *c.* 1230   20

A separation before execution: Experience of a Cathar (so-called
heretic) on being taken to an Inquisition tribunal, as reported
by Bishop Jacques Fournier, France, 13th century   20

Upsetting the order: Stephen, aged twelve, led a crowd of
30,000 into Paris in the 13th century in a 'children's crusade'.
This is the response of the French king, Philip II   21

The quaynte games of a wanton chylde: From *The Worlde and
the Childe*, a play of *c.* 1400 (anon.)   21

Don't pick your nose: Some advice by John Lydgate to a boy
serving at table, England, *c.* 1400   22

When my Dad was a boy . . .: Giovanni di Pagolo Morelli,
Italy, *c.* 1400   23

Me and my mates: From *L'Espinette Amoureuse*, Froissart,
France, *c.* 1400   23

A moan: Giovanni Dominici, Italy, *c.* 1400   24

Please can I go to the . . .: *c.* 1450, England   24

Hobby-horse: Violante de Pretis, governess to the Gonzaga
girls, Italy, 1471 25

How to be mannerly: *A Goodly Child*, anon., England, *c.* 1478 25

Don't throw your bones on the floor: Some advice on manners
when a child is away from home, anon., *c.* 1480 26

The horrible English: Italian observer, England, *c.* 1500 28

Home tuition: Remembered by Jerome Cardan, Italy, *c.* 1500 29

Dirty bits: Etiquette for schoolboys, from J. L. Vives, *Dialogues*,
c. 1519 29

Beat him: Advice of Henry IV of France to his son's tutors,
16th century 30

I hate scole: Manuscript of *c.* 1530, England 30

Go to work: From an Act of Parliament passed in the reign of
Henry VIII 32

No more unfittinge festivals: Henry VIII's Proclamation,
22 July 1542 32

A gentle schoolmaster: Lady Jane Grey to Roger Ascham,
c. 1550, England 34

Bunking off: Roger Ascham, *The Scholemaster*, *c.* 1560 34

Child marriage: first night problems: John Bridge v Elizabeth
Bridge (born Ramsbotham), 1561, England 35

Child marriage: four in the bed: Chester, 1562 35

Child marriage: too young to agree: Chester, 1564 36

We hate maths: Verse (anonymous), 1570, England 36

The kids aren't worth much: Verse (anonymous), 16th century,
England 37

Slippery slope: Choirboys in winter, London, 1595 37

Wool-sorters useful: Report by Thomas Deloney, *c.* 1600,
England 37

Cock of the walk: Heroard, Henry IV's physician, recorded the
details of Louis XIII's infancy, here quoted and summarized
by Philippe Ariès, *c.* 1601, France 38

Royal toys: Louis XIII's amusements, France, 1601–8 40

Be kynd, Dad: Dorothy Plumpton, *c.* 1600, writing to her
father from her stepmother's mother's house, England   40

Beginnings: Childhood of Jean-Jacques Bouchard, *c.* 1601,
France   41

Girls can: Abilities of the young Lucy Hutchinson, born 1620,
England   41

Light blue touch paper . . .: An accident to Marmaduke
Rawdon, aged twelve in 1621, York, England, as reported in
The Life   42

Beasts: Report by Wimborne churchwardens, 1629, England   43

Kindergarten Latin: From the diary of Henry Slingsby, *c.* 1630,
England   43

A holy twelve-year-old: A letter from Samuel Mather, 1638,
America   44

Ship 'em off: A bequest for enforced transportation   44

Free of reason: The nature of children as seen by Thomas
Hobbes, *The Citizen*, 1642, England   45

Of the boy and the butterfly: A poem by John Bunyan, *c.* 1650   45

Sparing the rod: From the diaries of J. Erskine, *c.* 1650, Scotland   46

Four years without thrashing: From anon., *A Rich Closet of
Physical Secrets . . . The Child-Bearer's Cabinet*, 1652, England   47

Girls and dolls: From *Of Government and Obedience* by John Hall
of Richmond, London, 1654   47

Let's get giddy: From *Of Government and Obedience* by John Hall
of Richmond, London, 1654   48

Rudeness: From M. Needham, *A Discourse concerning Schools and
School-Masters*, London, 1663   48

A hoyting girl: I was educated by my mother: Lady Anne
Fanshawe, 1676, England   48

Breeching little ffrank: Letter from the grandmother of Francis
Guildford, aged six, to the boy's father (and her son) Lord
Chief Justice North, 10 October 1679, America   49

The death of Papa: From a recollection by Richard Steele
in 1677 from *The Tatler*, 6 June 1710, England   50

Sam worried: From the diary of Samuel Sewall, *c.* 1680,
Massachusetts, America   51

John, Mary, Betty, Tom and William: Robert Russel in
A Little Book for Children, London, *c.* 1696   51

Listen, Katy . . .: From the diary of Cotton Mather; a note
about four-year-old Katy, 1698, New England, America   52

God doesn't like vain sports: John Gratton, describing himself
at the age of ten, 17th century, America   53

Nothing fancy at the Wesleys: Susanna Wesley, mother of
John Wesley, *c.* 1700   53

At the temporary store for bodies in the graveyard: From the
diary of Harriet Spencer, aged eleven, *c.* 1700, after seeing
bodies dug up to make room for new ones   54

It's my book: Children's 'autograph', early 18th century,
America   54

Small ad.: Advertisement in *The Tatler*, 9–11 February 1709   55

Alex, Bob and wot I think: Textbook graffito, 1710, England   55

. . . and don't forget the . . .: Shopping list sent by a mother
to her husband, 1714, London   55

Against quarrelling and fighting: A poem by Isaac Watts, 1715   56

Grandpa speaks: A story from Nicolas Restif de la Bretonne,
aged four, France, 1739. It was confirmed by his mother,
he says.   57

Grown up: Lord Chesterfield to his son, 1741. (He wrote many
letters like this; presumably the advice was not taken.)   57

Dear Mum: Letter to his mother from Frederick Reynolds,
aged about seven, after two days at Westminster School,
London, *c.* 1750   58

How to be nice: Hugh Blair, *Lectures on Rhetoric*, *c.* 1750,
on advice to the well-bred youth   58

The drugs solution for children: From *A Treatise on Opium*
by George Young, MD, *c.* 1750   59

Dirty books: Memories of Rev. Thomas Scott of school in
the 1750s   59

Dear Dad: A schoolboy's letter, 1752, America   60

Captured: Olaudah Equiano in *c.* 1756 in what is now Eastern
Nigeria, from *The Interesting Narrative of the Life of Olaudah
Equiano or Gustavus Vassa the African*, published 1789   60

Spoilt American kids: Report of an English gentleman returning
home after a visit to America, *Virginia Gazette*, 1767   63

The non-believer: From the diary of James Boswell, *c.* 1770   64

All dressed up: Account by Anna Green Winslow, aged twelve,
1771, America   64

Trying to be diligent: A letter from John Quincy Adams,
aged nine, to his father, President John Adams, America   65

The dreamer: School memories of Samuel Taylor Coleridge,
c. 1778, England   66

An old Scots remedy: Memories of Sir Walter Scott, *c.* 1780,
from Lockhart's *Life of Scott*, 1845, Scotland   67

The school dungeons: Childhood memories of Charles Lamb in
1782, from *Christ's Hospital Five and Thirty Years Ago*, England   68

A home entertainment: A record of the childhood of Robert
Southey (1774–1823), England   69

Every man his place in life: A Church Minister's view of
education, 1785, England   69

National order: Report in *The Times*, London, 1788   70

The problem with slaves: The strictures of a Virginia judge,
18th century   70

Good and bad: From the 'Monitor' or diary of Mary Osgood
Sumner, her lists of 'Black Leaf' (bad deeds) and 'White
Leaf' (good deeds). Georgia, 18th century   71

Dad as a boy: A young lady's account of her father's schooldays
in the late 18th century   73

An educational sandhill: From *Rural Rides* by William Cobbett,
published in England in 1830   74

A vision: A childhood experience of William Blake, *c.* 1800   75

Keep your clothes on: From an anonymous manual of
household government, early 19th century, America   75

Goodbye, little bastard: From a letter from Charles Lamb, writer, early 19th century 77

Curing prostitution in the colony: Governor King reports to the Duke of Portland, Sydney, Australia, 1802 77

Keep the clothes decent: From *A Familiar View of the Domestic Education of Children,* by Dr Christian Augustus Struve, 1802 78

A less than useful wall: William Hutton, five years old in 1805, from *Life,* 1882 78

Scenes of our childhood: Written by the English poet John Clare (1793–1864) when he was ten years old 79

A delightful dawdle: From the diary of Ellen Weeton, *c.* 1807 81

A little devil: From the diary of Marjory Fleming, aged seven, in 1810, England 81

A good teacher: School memories of Mary Sewell, 1882 82

Memories and feelings: Three extracts from the autobiography of Harriet Martineau (1802–76), published in England in 1877 83

Busy day: A day at a London elementary school, 1814 84

Slave-girl: An account by Elizabeth Keckley of life in Virginia and North Carolina, *c.* 1820, from *Behind the Scenes, or, Thirty Years a Slave, and Four Years in the White House,* 1868 85

A friendly word of advice: A recollection by Samuel Smiles, *c.* 1822, England 87

Great writer's secret love: Charles Dickens (1812–70) 87

Female tasks: Sign in an American orphanage in the 1820s 87

Making a living: From an unpublished memoir (written 1865) by Joseph Terry, aged six in *c.* 1822 88

Sufficient possessions: From John Ruskin's *Præterita* (published 1899), a recollection from *c.* 1825 89

The road-mender's family: Report on Labourers' Wages, 1824 90

A heavy punishment: Evidence of Ellen Hootton, aged ten in 1833, from the Parliamentary Commission inquiry into the state of children in mines and manufactories 90

Funny uniform: A letter from Charlotte Yonge, aged eleven,
to her cousin Anne, 1834, England   91

A scientist: Observations by Emily Shore, aged eleven, 1835,
England   92

Guilt: From the autobiography of George Mockford, aged ten
in *c.* 1836   93

A twelve-year-old convict: A Frenchman in the commissariat
at Port Arthur, Australia, cites a convict case, 1839   94

A coal-miner: From evidence of Margaret Leveston, aged six,
East Scotland, 1842, for the Parliamentary Commission
inquiry into the state of children in mines and manufactories   95

Pranks: A letter from Charles Dodgson (Lewis Carroll),
aged twelve, at boarding school, to his sisters, 1844,
England   95

A first memory: Edmund Gosse in *c.* 1852, England   96

The collector: Edmund Gosse, aged nine, in 1858, England,
from *Father and Son* (published 1907)   96

A real sin: Coventry Patmore, *c.* 1860   97

A treasure island: Robert Louis Stevenson, *c.* 1860, in
Child's Play, Scotland, 1881   97

Backstreet care: 'An Orphan Girl, A Street-Seller'   98

Ducking and diving: 'A Mudlark', aged about thirteen,
an Irish boy from Kerry, in London   99

Excuses, excuses: Logbook from a London elementary girls'
school   100

Bug-lore: An American child's experience in the 1860s   101

Beloved children: An advertisement in *The Times*, 16 February
1864   102

Eton beating: Account by J. Brinsley-Richards, then aged ten,
in *Seven Years at Eton*, in *c.* 1867, England   102

A good education: Beatrix Potter (1866–1943), writing in 1940   103

Many happy hours: Advertisement, England, 1879   104

He learned the boy: A school tale from Charlie Wickett,
in 1889, Cornwall, England   104

A frightening king: Memories of a Japanese schoolboy, 1890s,
Tokyo   105

A silly little girl: From *The Girl's Own Paper*, 28 July 1894,
England   106

A punishment: Twentieth-century punishment   106

The man's way: An experience recounted by David Garnett in
The Golden Echo, *c*. 1900, England   107

What they say: Children's sayings recorded in 1900   107

The bedroom: From the unpublished autobiography
of Jack Lanigan (born 1890); experiences at the age
of about ten   108

Family life: From unpublished memoirs of Faith Dorothy
Osgerby, aged about ten in 1900   108

Not knowing Noah: At Sunday school, recounted by
Ada Cambridge, in Victoria, Australia, 1903   110

A warm new sensation: Ethel Mannin in 1906, England;
from *Confessions and Impressions*, 1930   110

Song: Zulu girls' song   111

The tooth-bird: Zulu children's custom   111

Zulu backslang: Gazaland   112

Australian cowboy: Colin Bingham in northern Queensland,
Australia, 1906–7   112

Kangaroo hunter: 'The butcher's daughter', rural Western
Australia, *c*. 1907   113

An Edwardian childhood: An interview with Jessie Niblett,
c. 1908, Bristol, England   114

Is it a dolly?: The humorist Stephen Potter on kindergarten
days   116

Out of bondage: Childhood in Hunan, China, *c*. 1910   117

Orphan Ivy: An interview with Ivy Petherick, at Muller's
Orphanage from 1910, aged nine   120

Washday: From an unpublished memoir by Bessie Wallis,
aged six in *c*. 1910   121

Children's strike: Larry Goldstone recounting a revolt of
Manchester schoolchildren, September 1911, in a letter to
Stephen Humphries   122

She's in the Sally Army: Song of children passing Salvation
Army parade before the First World War   123

Sudden death?: Lilian Campbell, Melbourne, Australia, before
the First World War   124

The golf links: A poem by Sarah N. Cleghorn, 1915, America   124

Dealing with a truant: Interview with Frank Unwin at
Highfields Industrial School, near Liverpool, during the
First World War   125

Bottom: From an autobiography by Edith Hall, aged seven
in 1915   126

Absolute silence: Cyril Hayward-Jones at The Mount School
for the Deaf and Blind near Stoke-on-Trent, England, *c.* 1916   127

Polio: Alice Maguire, in Norfolk, England, *c.* 1916   127

An alternative view: An interview with Jim Flowers, Bristol,
England, 1918   128

The Brownies: From the handbook for Guides written by
Sir Robert Baden-Powell, KCB, KCVO, LLD, founder of the
Scout movement   129

Finding out about steam: Dorothy Scannell (Dolly
Chegwidden), *c.* 1920, London   131

Afraid of passing exams: Interview with Sam Emberey,
near Yeovil, England, 1920s   131

The hiring fair: Interview with Rose McCullach, aged thirteen,
Strabane, Ireland, in 1922   133

On an Aboriginal penal settlement: Experiences of
Marnie Kennedy, Palm Island, Australia, in the 1920s,
from *Born a Half-Caste*   134

A Maori girl's first day at school: Mihi Edwards, aged six,
in New Zealand, 1924   135

Sex education: Interview with Connie Denby, Sheffield,
England, in the 1920s   135

Why?: Questions . . ., 1927   136

More whys: Factual 'why' questions, recorded by Susan Isaacs, a child psychologist, 1930   136

In New Guinea: The preoccupations of young people, 1930   137

Never for killing's sake: Kath Walker (Oodgeroo Noonuccal), Stradbroke Island, Queensland, Australia, *c.* 1930   139

Late again, boy: From an interview with Bill Bees, Gloucestershire, England, 1930s   142

Cursed: David Swift, born with an hereditary muscular disease, Nottingham, England, 1930s   143

Bloody Jew: Zelda D'Aprano, Melbourne, Australia, in the 1930s   144

Waiting for the baby: Extracts from the account of Ursula during her mother's pregnancy   145

Splints: From a mother's letter, 1933   148

Not her fault: 'Information from a woman acquaintance' of Susan Isaacs, child psychologist, 1933, England   149

A good game: From a letter to Susan Isaacs, child psychologist, 1933, England   150

Closely observed: Incidents in the lives of children aged between two years eight months and four years eleven months, from professional backgrounds   150

The twins: Experiences of Moshe Offer, aged twelve in 1944   153

The root of all evil: Story from a friend of Walter de la Mare, England, 1949   155

Circumcision: An account from the 1950s, Bethany, Palestine   156

A joke: Recorded by an American psychologist   157

An experiment: The 1950s in a state school for mentally handicapped children in Massachusetts, reported in the *Boston Globe* and then the *Guardian*, 6 January 1994   158

Revolutionary priorities: An experience of Jung Chang in China, 1950s   159

My friend Billy: A playground rhyme by a ten-year-old girl,
Northern Ireland, 1958   160

Toast: A poem by Maureen Natt, England, 1970s   160

November 1975: A conversation between Natasha, aged six,
and Adam, aged eight, recorded by R. D. Laing   161

Hunch Bunch: A playground rhyme by a girl aged twelve,
London, 1977   162

Coming home: A poem by Brenda Dundas, aged thirteen,
London, 1977   163

What parents say: Parents' irritating sayings, collected
by children aged twelve and thirteen at Toot Hill
Comprehensive School, Bingham, Nottinghamshire,
England, 1978   163

In the playground: Children describe their new song-and-dance
to Iona Opie, England, 1978   164

In the news: Iona Opie records children in a playground   166

Moving in: A poem by Marisa Horsford, aged ten,
Nottingham, 1970s   167

Every morning: A poem by Keith Ballentine, aged twelve,
London, 1979   168

Moon man: Five-year-olds talking, America, 1981   168

Greed: A poem by John Hegley   170

One of the wise men: Black children in a Nativity play:
Gary Younge, *Guardian*, 1993   170

Mam: A poem to her mother by Mary Bell, aged thirteen,
two years after being convicted of the manslaughter of
two boys, aged four and three, 1970   171

Sunday school teacher: Poem by Robin, aged ten, England,
1972   172

A hero: Five-year-olds talking, America, 1981   173

Santa Claus: Five-year-olds talking, America, 1981   174

The tooth gazelle: Iraqi boy's account of what to do when
a child loses a tooth, 1981   175

Getting the point: A group of American five-year-olds, 1981   176

Bad guy: Four-year-olds in Chicago, America, 1980s 177

Skipping song: A song by ten-year-old girls in Harlem,
New York City, in the 1980s, collected by Karol Swanson 180

S-t-r-e-t-c-h-i-n-g: A poem by Sharon Cheeks, aged about ten,
London, 1982 180

My memories: A poem by Tanweer Khaled, aged about twelve,
London, 1984 181

Understanding: Leanne Platek, in Staffordshire, aged eleven,
during the Miners' Strike, Great Britain, 1984–5 182

Bed!: A poem by Joni Akinrele from Benthal Primary School,
Hackney, London, 1984 182

Why?: A poem by Ben Bruton, Wood's Foundation Church of
England School, 1985 183

Freedom: A poem by Moagi, aged about seven, South Africa,
1980s 184

Song: A playground rhyme by girls aged seven, London, 1985 184

Typically middle-class: Sarah Hobson reporting in 'Battered
and abused children', Great Britain, 1980s 185

I a boy one witch: Sarah Hobson reporting in 'Battered
and abused children', Great Britain, 1980s 188

A dream: A poem by Ho Foong Ling, aged about ten,
Singapore, 1985 189

Detention: Anne Chisholm in 'Children in prison', on an
Indian 'child care home', 1980s 190

On the streets: An account by Andrea di Robilant of street
children in Brazil, 1980s 191

Song: A playground song from a London girl aged seven, 1985 191

Toi-toi: Related by a teacher in Western Cape, South Africa,
1986 193

I warned you: A story related by a boy aged nine, London,
1989 193

Punk boy: Poem by Basid, aged ten, Bethnal Green, London,
1989 195

The fib: A journalist reports on lying   195
. . . and when he . . .: Samantha, Justine and Colette discuss
Honey, I Shrunk the Kids, London, 1993   196
The pregnancy: A newspaper report   198

A Year's Headlines   201
Acknowledgements   209
References   212

Introduction

We live in a time when the anxiety about *what children might turn into* couldn't be higher, but the interest in *childhood* is as low as it has ever been. Though most of us meet, see and talk with children all the time, they are also presented to us as icons and symbols. The news media are mostly interested in children as victims. In my experience, monitoring a week's newspapers, say, for stories about children, reveals that over 90 per cent show children as battered, abused and murder victims. This chorus is interrupted only by accounts of children's evil and advertisements where they appear as smiling clothes-hangers.

Children are also visible (just) in the now-desperate struggle over education. Concealed beneath the battle is a disagreement about attitudes to childhood: on the one hand, there are people who see education in terms of the finished product, and on the other, there are those who consider that if the process feels right, the outcome will be right too. The so-called 'progressive' school of thought came out of many years' study of what children seem to think and do. The new educational orthodoxy, as represented in the National Curriculum documents for England and Wales, has no time for speculation on childhood. It is interesting that we use the same word for the educational process as we do for horse-racing – a course; a predetermined sequence of obstacles that will be negotiated by all participants; anyone falling will be eliminated; only the first three give returns on bets.

There is also a representation of childhood that sees children as a separate tribe. Clearly, in our culture they are frequently put into child enclosures, the playground or the children's television programme, and we distinguish ourselves from children through words like 'immature' and 'childish'. We then express anxieties about this undeveloped state through concerns about safety and sex. There is something intractably circular about a culture that denies children power and produces people who abuse children. This abuse is rightly condemned, yet is usually seen as unrelated to the ways the culture controls and limits children.

This anthology, then, has a bias; it tries to show both the ways in which children have been controlled as well as ways in which they prove their capabilities. I have been interested to find early examples of behaviour we might think of as modern, and likewise, examples of behaviour once sanctioned but now thought of as impossible or wrong. Our concern about the present era arises in part from our tendency to construct imaginary golden ages. These mingle with notions of childhood and so I have tried to show some un-golden moments to counterbalance the usual codswallop.

There is also a detectable bias in the matter of provenance. The literate, the educated and indeed the literary are extremely well documented in previous views and collections of childhood. In fact, it could be said that one of the main sources for literary inspiration has been that well of feeling, childhood. I have tended to lean away from this area, not entirely though, in the hopes of showing a less familiar picture.

The sub-text to all this theorizing is that I think childhood is lived in very different ways, depending on place, time and culture. I have failed to express as wide a range as I would have liked, but I am not multilingual, and to do so would have needed the work of more than one person, living in more than one place. However, by showing some diversity and contrast with the customary, I have tried to imply that childhood is as variegated as . . . well, adulthood.

Dad knows best

Ancient Egypt (New Kingdom), 2000–1500 BC

On another happy occasion you grasp the meaning of a papyrus roll ... You begin to read a book, you quickly make calculations. Let no sound of your mouth be heard; write with your hand, read with your mouth. Ask from those who know more than you, and don't be weary. Spend no day in idleness, or woe to your body. Try to understand what your teacher wants, listen to his instructions. Be a scribe! 'Here I am,' you will say, every time he calls you.

•

Pupil to teacher

Ancient Egypt (New Kingdom), 2000–1500 BC

I grew up beside you, you smote my back, and so your teaching entered my ear.

•

Grave message

Inscription on the tomb of Thothrekh,
Ancient Egypt, Late Period (1000 BC–AD 100)

Who hears my speech, his heart will grieve for it,
For I am a small child snatched by force,
Abridged in years as an innocent one,

Snatched quickly as a little one,
Like a man carried off by sleep.
I was a youngster of – years,
When taken to the city of eternity,
To the abode of the perfect souls;
I therefore reached the Lord of Gods,
Without having had my share.

I was rich in friends,
All the men of my town,
Not one of them could protect me!
All the town's people, men and women,
Lamented very greatly,
Because they saw what happened to me,
For they esteemed me much.
All my friends mourned for me,
Father and Mother implored Death;
My brothers, they were head-on-knee,
Since I reached this land of deprivation.
When people were reckoned before the Lord of Gods,
No fault (of mine) was found;
I received bread in the hall of the Two Truths,
Water from the sycamore as (one of) the perfect souls.

•

What to do with boys

Protagoras (*c*. 485–*c*. 415 BC),
Ancient Greece

If he is willing, he obeys, but if not, they straighten him, just
like a bent and twisted piece of wood, with threats and blows.

•

Girls play 'The Tortoise'

A game of Ancient Greece

Girls played *khelikhelōnē*, 'tortoise', a tag game . . .: the 'tortoise'
– an animal associated with the home, woolworking, and the
love of children – sits in the middle while other girls circle her,
engaging in a series of queries and replies which ends with her
attempt to catch one of them:

> Tortoise, what are you doing in the middle?
> I'm weaving wool and Milesian thread.
> What was your son doing when he died?
> From white horses into the sea he was – jumping.

●

Iphis speaks

Euripides (480–406 BC), from *Suppliant Women*, Ancient Greece

There is nothing more joyful to an aged father than a daughter.
Boys have greater courage, but are less given to sweet endearments.

●

Creon speaks

Sophocles (496–406 BC), Ancient Greece

Put everything second to a father's opinion. It is for this that men pray to have obedient children in their homes, to pay back evil to their father's enemy and honor his friend as he does.

•

Decline in standards

Socrates (469–399 BC)

From the day your baby is born, you must teach him to do without things. Children today love luxury too much. They have execrable manners, flaunt authority, have no respect for their elders. They no longer rise when their parents or teachers enter the room. What kind of awful creatures will they be when they grow up?

•

Bedwetting explained

Lucretius, from *De Rerum Natura*, c. 80 BC

> . . . Kids wet the bed
> Soaking not only sheets, but also spreads,
> Magnificent Babylonian counterpanes,
> Because it seemed that in their dreams they stood
> Before a urinal or chamber pot
> With lifted nightgowns.

•

A brave girl

Pliny (*c.* AD 23–79), on the death of a girl,
Ancient Rome

How she used to hang from her father's neck! How lovingly
and modestly she embraced us as her father's friends! How she
used to love her nurses, *paedagogi*, and teachers as was appropriate to the status of each of them! With how much effort and
intelligence did she used to read! How rarely and carefully
would she play! With what self-control, patience, and constancy
did she bear her final illness! She encouraged the physicians,
exhorted her sister and her father, and kept herself going
through the strength of her spirit when the power of her body
had deserted her.

•

The beastly foreigners

Plutarch on the Carthaginians, writing *c.* AD 50

... with full knowledge and understanding they themselves
offered up their own children, and those who had no children
would buy little ones from poor people and cut their throats as
if they were so many lambs or young birds; meanwhile the
mother stood by without a tear or moan; but should she utter a
single moan or let fall a single tear, she had to forfeit the
money, and her child was sacrificed nevertheless; and the whole
area before the statue was filled with a loud noise of flutes and
drums so that the cries of wailing should not reach the ears of
the people.

•

Castration not complex

Paulus Aegineta, Ancient Rome

... children, still of a tender age, are placed in a vessel of hot water, and then when the parts are softened in the bath, the testicles are to be squeezed with the fingers until they disappear.

•

Romans on childhood

Marcus Aurelius (AD 121–80)

We give children proverbs – what the Greeks call *chriai* – to learn off by heart, since the childish mind which cannot yet comprehend anything more can nevertheless grasp such proverbs.

Seneca (*c.* 4 BC–AD 65)

He used to be a child: he has become adult. That is a difference of quality. For the child is irrational, the adult rational.

Cicero (106–43 BC)

The thing itself [childhood] cannot be praised, only its potential.

•

Mutilating children for freak shows

Seneca, writing *c.* AD 50

Look on the blind wandering about the streets leaning on their sticks, and those with crushed feet, and still again look on those with broken limbs. This one is without arms, that one has had his shoulders pulled down out of shape in order that his grotesqueries may excite laughter ... let us go to the origin of all those ills – a laboratory for the manufacture of human wrecks – a cavern filled with the limbs torn from living children ... What wrong has been done to the Republic? On the contrary, have not these children been done a service inasmuch as their parents had cast them out?

•

Vipstanus Messalla complains

Tacitus in *Dialogus de Oratoribus, c.* AD 100

Nowadays, at birth our children are handed over to some silly little Greek serving girl and some male slave or other – typically the most worthless fellow in the whole household, someone not suited for any kind of serious work. From the very outset they fill the children's tender and gullible minds with their stuff and nonsense, and not one person in the entire establishment gives a thought to what he should say or do in the presence of his infant master. Moreover, even the parents themselves accustom their offspring to lewdness and glib talk in lieu of goodness and modesty, as a result of which they gradually lose their sense of shame and become equally contemptuous of themselves and others.

•

Ducks and drakes

Minucius Felix, near Rome, *c.* AD 300

Then our party came to a place where several small boats, having been drawn up on the shore, rested above ground on oaken rollers so as to prevent rot. There we saw a group of small boys, who were eagerly vying with one another in a game of ducks and drakes. This is what the game is all about: you choose a well-rounded shell from the shore – one that has been rubbed smooth by the pounding of the waves – and holding it horizontally in your fingers while stooping as low to the ground as you can get, you send it spinning across the water. Once thrown, it should either skim the surface of the sea, gliding smoothly along, or conversely shave the tops of the waves, only to resurface time and time again. Among the boys, the one whose shell has gone the farthest and skipped the most declares himself the winner.

•

Dear Dad . . .

Letter written in Greece, *c.* AD 300

Theon to his father Theon, greeting. Thank you for not taking me to town with you. If you won't take me with you to Alexandria I won't write you a letter or speak to you or say goodbye to you; and if you go to Alexandria I won't take your hand nor greet you again. That is what will happen if you won't take me. Mother said to Archelaus, 'He drives me crazy: take him.' Thank you for sending me presents . . . Send for me, *please*. If you don't I won't eat, I won't drink; there now!

•

Naughty

From St Augustine's *Confessions, c.* AD 364

There was a pear-tree near our vineyard, loaded with fruit that was attractive neither to look at nor to taste. Late one night a band of ruffians, myself included, went off to shake down the fruit and carry it away, for we had continued our games out of doors until well after dark, as was our pernicious habit. We took away an enormous quantity of pears, not to eat them ourselves, but simply to throw them to the pigs. Perhaps we ate some of them, but our real pleasure consisted in doing something that was forbidden.

•

Granddad's words of wisdom

Ausonius, Gallic professor of rhetoric,
to his six-year-old grandson, 4th century

Learn willingly, dear grandson, do not curse the control of that grim teacher. Never shudder at the teacher's appearance. His age may make him frightening, and his harsh words and frowning brows may lead you to think that he wants to pick a quarrel with you – but once you've trained your face to remain impassive, he will never again seem an ogre.

•

Boy-kings are a pain

Historian, Rome, *c.* AD 500

May the gods save us from boy-emperors and from proclaiming children 'Fathers of the Community' and from those whose alphabet-teachers have to guide their hands when it comes to signing documents, who are persuaded to make consular appointments by sweets and toys and whatever gives children pleasure.

•

At the school for monks

Aelfric, *Colloquy*, Cerne Abbas, England, *c.* AD 900

Master . . . You, boy, what did you do today?
Pupil I did lots of things. Last night when I heard the ringing of the bell I got up from my bed and went to church and sang matins with the brethren, after which we sang of all the saints and the morning hymns; after this the six o'clock service and the seven psalms with the litanies and the chapter-Eucharist. Then we sang the nine o'clock service and did the Eucharist for the day; after this we sang the midday service, and ate and drank and slept. And we got up again and sang the three o'clock service; and now we are here before you, ready to hear what you have to say to us!
Master When are you going to sing evensong and compline?
Pupil When it's time!
Master Have you been beaten today?
Pupil I haven't, because I behave myself carefully.
Master And how about your friends?
Pupil Why do you ask me about that? I dare not reveal our

secrets to you. Each one of us knows if he was beaten or not.

Master What do you eat in the day?

Pupil I still enjoy meat, because I am a child living under instruction.

Master What else do you eat?

Pupil I eat vegetables and eggs, fish and cheese, butter and beans and all clean things, with much gratefulness.

Master You are very greedy if you eat everything that is in front of you.

Pupil I am not so great a glutton that I can eat all kinds of food at one meal.

Master Then how so?

Pupil Sometimes I partake of this food and sometimes that, in moderation as befits a monk, not with greed, because I am no glutton.

Master And what do you drink?

Pupil Ale if I have it, or water if I have no ale.

Master Don't you drink wine?

Pupil I'm not rich enough to buy myself wine; and wine isn't a drink for children or the foolish, but for the old and wise.

Master Where do you sleep?

Pupil In the dormitory with the brothers.

Master Who wakes you up for matins?

Pupil Sometimes I hear the ringing of the bell and get up; sometimes my teacher wakes me sternly with a cane.

Master Well, you boys and charming scholars, your teacher reminds you to be obedient to the commandments of God, and to behave yourselves properly everywhere. When you hear the church bells, go in an orderly fashion and go into the church and bow humbly towards the holy altars, and stand up properly, and sing in unison, and pray for your sins; and go out into the cloisters or to study without playing the fool.

•

In the sand-pit

From the autobiography of Gerald of Wales, *c.* 1155

Giraldus was born in South Wales on the sea-coast of Dyfed, not far from the chief town of Pembroke, in the Castle of Manorbier ... He was the youngest of four brothers ... and when the other three, preluding the pursuits of manhood in their childish play, were tracing or building, in sand or dust, now towns, now palaces, he himself, in like prophetic play, was ever busy with all his might in designing churches or building monasteries. And his father, who often saw him thus engaged, after much pondering, not unmixed with wonder, being moved by this omen, resolved with wise forethought to set him to study letters and the liberal arts, and would oft in approving jest call him 'his Bishop'.

•

Fear of candles

William of Malmesbury writing in the 12th century
about Ethelred the Unready (born *c.* 969)

I have read that when he was ten years of age and heard the report that his brother [Edward the Martyr] was killed, he so irritated his furious mother by his weeping that she, not having a whip at hand, beat the little innocent with some candles she snatched up, nor did she desist until he was drenched with tears and nearly lifeless. For this reason he dreaded candles for the rest of his life, so much so that he would never let their light be brought into his presence.

•

Are they not human?

Eadmer, England, *c.* 1100

One day, when a certain Abbot, much reputed for his piety, spake with Anselm concerning divers points of Monastic Religion, and conversed among other things of the boys that were brought up in the cloister, he added: 'What, pray, can we do with them? They are perverse and incorrigible; day and night we cease not to chastise them, yet they grow daily worse and worse.' Whereat Anselm marvelled, and said, 'Ye cease not to beat them? And when they are grown to manhood, of what sort are they then?' 'They are dull and brutish,' said the other. Then said Anselm, 'With what good profit do ye expend your substance in nurturing human beings till they become brute beasts?' 'Nay,' said the other, 'but what else can we do? By all means we compel them to profit, yet our labour is unprofitable.' 'Ye *compel* them, my lord Abbot? Tell me, I prithee, if thou shouldst plant a sapling in thy garden, and presently shut it in on all sides so that it could nowhere extend its branches; when thou hadst liberated it after many years, what manner of tree would come forth? Would it not be wholly unprofitable, with gnarled and tangled branches? And whose fault would it be but thine own, who hadst closed it in beyond all reason. Thus without doubt do ye with your children. They have been planted in the Garden of the Church by way of Oblation, there to grow and bear fruit to God. But ye so hem them in on every side with terrors, threats, and stripes, that they can get no liberty whatsoever; wherefore, being thus indiscreetly afflicted, they put forth a tangle of evil thoughts like thorns, which they so foster and nourish, and thus bring to so thick a growth, that their obstinate minds become impenetrable to all possible threats for their correction. Hence it cometh to pass that, perceiving in you no love for themselves, no pity, no kindness, no gentleness, they are unable henceforth to trust in your goodness, believing rather that all your works are done through hatred and envy against them; insomuch that (I grieve to say it), even as they grow in stature, so doth this hatred and suspicion of all evil grow with them; for evil ever bendeth and glideth downward and downward into vice. Wherefore, having nowhere found true charity in their bringing-up, they cannot look upon any man but with scowling brow and sidelong glance. But I prithee tell me, for God's sake, wherefore ye are so set against them? Are they not human, sharing in the same nature as yourselves? Would ye wish to be so handled as ye handle them? Ye will say, "Yes, if we were as they are." So be it, then; yet is there no way but that of stripes and scourges for shaping them to good? Did ye ever see a goldsmith shape his gold or silver plate into a fair image by blows alone? I trow not. What then? That he may give the plate its proper shape, he will first press it gently and tap it with his tools; then again he will more softly raise it with discreet pressure from below, and caress it into shape. So ye also, if ye would see your boys adorned with fair manners, ye should not only beat them down with stripes, but also raise their spirits and support them with fatherly kindness and pity.'

•

She loves me, she loves me not . . .

Walther von der Vogelweider, Holland or Germany, *c.* 1200

> A spire of grass hath made me gay –
> I measured in the self-same way
> I have seen practised by a child.
> Come, look, and listen if she really does,
> She does, does not, she does, does not, she does.

•

Equality some way off

Paulo of Certaldo, Middle Ages

. . . nourish the sons well. How you nourish the daughter does not matter as long as you keep her alive.

•

Justice

Philip of Beaumanoir, end of 13th century

. . . if such a child [10–12 years old] commits a murder of his own free will or as an agent of some other person he is to be executed.

•

Body contact in the monastery

Custumal of Bec, Middle Ages

Let the masters sleep between every two boys in the dormitory, and sit between every two at other times, and, if it be night, let all the candles be fixed without on the spikes which crown the lanterns, that they may be plainly seen in all that they do. When they lie down in bed, let a master always be among them with his rod and (if it be night) with a candle, holding the rod in one hand and the light in the other. If any chance to linger after the rest, he is forthwith smartly touched; for children everywhere need custody with discipline and discipline with custody. And be it known that this is all their discipline, either to be beaten with rods, or that their hair should be stoutly plucked; never are they disciplined with kicks, or fists, or the open hand, or in any other way . . .

When they wash, let masters stand between each pair at the lavatory . . . When they sit in cloister or chapter, let each have his own tree-trunk for a seat, and so far apart that none touch in any way even the skirt of the other's robe . . . let them wipe their hands as far as possible one from the other, that is, at opposite corners of the towel . . .

•

Medieval romping

Cuvelier, France, Middle Ages

[The Knight] Renaud du Guesclin was Bertrand's father, and his mother a most gentle lady and most comely; but for the boy of whom I tell you, methinks there was none so hideous from

Rennes to Dinant. Flat-nosed he was and dark of skin, heavy and froward; wherefore his parents hated him so sore that often in their hearts they wished him dead, or drowned in some swift stream; *Rascal*, *Fool*, or *Clown* they were wont to call him; so despised was he, as an ill-conditioned child, that squires and servants made light of him; but we have oftentimes seen, in this world of vain shadows, that the most despised have been the greatest . . .

So when he had fulfilled eight or nine years, he took a custom of his own, as I will here tell. Many a time and oft he would go play in the fields, gathering around him forty or fifty boys, whom he would divide into companies and make them fight as at a tournament – yea, and so fiercely that one would rudely overthrow the other. When therefore Bertrand saw his fellows overthrown before his face, to their great hurt, then would he run and help them to rise, saying, 'Haste now, avenge yourself well and boldly on that other!' Thus he skilfully kept up the fight and the tourney by thrusting himself among them; as hounds tear wolves with their teeth, so he would overthrow even the great ones and bruise them sore, and they knew him by this token, that all his clothes were torn and his body bleeding. Truly I declare that he made no account of his own blood; thus would he cry aloud, 'Guesclin to the rescue!' and maintain the fight so long that none knew which side had the victory. When therefore all were glutted with fighting, then he would bid them cease, and say in a soft voice: 'Come, good fellows all, let us go privily and drink all together as good friends; I will pay, so long as there is a penny in my purse.'

•

A bit young for the job

From *Exempla*, stories for the use of preachers,
by Jacques de Vitry, Paris, *c.* 1230

How wretched and mad are those men who commit the cure of
many thousand souls to their little nephews whom they would
not trust with three pears, lest they should eat them! I have
heard how one of these boys, after receiving an archdeaconry
from a bishop his uncle, was set solemnly in his stall during the
ceremony of installation, and was found not yet to have out-
grown the needful ministrations of his nurse.

•

A separation before execution

Experience of a Cathar (so-called heretic) on
being taken to an Inquisition tribunal, as reported by
Bishop Jacques Fournier, France, 13th century

She had an infant in his cradle and she wanted to see him before
leaving home. On seeing him, she kissed him and the infant
began to smile. She began to move away from the cradle in
order to leave the room, but retraced her footsteps and again
approached the infant. He again smiled and the same happened
several times. He held her by his smile, and she could not leave
him. In the end, she said to the maidservant 'take him out of the
room'.

•

Upsetting the order

Stephen, aged twelve, led a crowd of 30,000 into Paris
in the 13th century in a 'children's crusade'.
This is the response of the French king, Philip II.

My child, you claim to serve God's natural order better than we
do, but you are mistaken. For in this order parents command
children, priests bless, knights fight, peasants labour and children obey. If we let children preach and command, do you not
see that the order is reversed? The devil has led you into a trap
and you have fallen into it.

●

The quaynte games of a wanton chylde

From *The Worlde and the Childe*,
a play of *c.* 1400 (anon.)

Aha, wanton is my name:
I can many a quaynte game.
Lo my toppe I dryve in same,
Se it torneth rounde:

I can daunce and also skyppe,
I can playe at the chery pytte,
And I can wystell you a fytte,
Syres, in a whylowe ryne:
Ye, syrs, and every daye,
Whan I to scole shall take the waye
Some good mannes gardyn I wyll assaye,
Perys and plommes to plucke.
I can spye a sparowes nest,

I will not go to scole but whan me lest,
For there begynneth a sory fest,
When the mayster sholde lyfte my docke.

Notes:

I can wystell you a fytte,
... in a whylowe ryne:
I can whistle you a bar [of music]
... in a [hollowed-out] willow stick
perys: pears
whan me lest: when it pleases me

•

Don't pick your nose

Some advice by John Lydgate to a boy serving at table, England, *c.* 1400

My dear child, first thyself enable
With all thine heart to virtuous discipline;
Afore thy sovereign, standing at the table,
Dispose thou thee after my doctrine
To all nurture thy courage to incline.
First, when thou speakest be not reckless,
Keep feet and fingers still in peace.
Be simple of cheer, cast not thine eye aside,
Gaze not about, turning thy sight over all.
Against the post let not thy back abide,
Neither make thy mirror of the wall.
Pick not thy nose, and, most especial,
Be well ware, and set hereon thy thought,
Before thy sovereign scratch nor rub thee nought.

•

When my Dad was a boy . . .

Giovanni di Pagolo Morelli, Italy, *c.* 1400

Impelled by his good character he went to school of his own
accord to learn to read and write ... When he had received
many blows from his teacher he left and wouldn't go back. And
so by himself, without any intermediary, he changed teachers
many times and with some (as he later told his wife) he would
make a bargain and get a promise not to be beaten. If the
bargain was kept he stayed, if not, he departed.

•

Me and my mates

From *L'Espinette Amoureuse*, Froissart, France, *c.* 1400

In that early childish day
I was never tired to play
Games that children everyone
Love until twelve years are done.
To dam up a rivulet
With a tile, or else to let
A small saucer for a boat
Down the purling gutter float:
Over two bricks at a will
To erect a water mill.

In those days for dice and chess
Cared we busy children less
Than mud-pies and buns to make,
And heedfully in oven bake.
Of four bricks; and when came Lent

Out was brought a complement
Of river shells from secret hold,
Estimated above gold,
To play away as I thought meet
With the children of our street.

•

A moan

Giovanni Dominici, Italy, *c.* 1400

How much time is wasted in the frequent combing of children's hair; in keeping the hair blond if they are girls or perhaps having it curled! How much care is taken to teach them how to have a good time, to make courtesies and bows; how much inanity and expense in the making of embroidered bonnets, ornamented capes, fancy petticoats, carved cradles, little colored shoes and fine hose!

•

Please can I go to the . . .

c. 1450, England

As sone on as I am cum into the schole, this fellow goith to make water.

•

Hobby-horse

Violante de Pretis, governess to the Gonzaga girls,
Italy, 1471

They are anxious to learn, and even to work. When they desire
to amuse themselves, they mount their little horse, one on the
saddle, the other pillion behind her, while a man on horseback
keeps pace with them.

•

How to be mannerly

A Goodly Child, anon., England, *c.* 1478

It is to a goodly child well fitting
        To use disports of mirth and pleasance,
To harp, or lute, or lustily to sing,
        Or in the press right mannerly to dance.
        When men see a child of such governance
        They say, 'Glad may this child's friends be
        To have a child so mannerly as he.'

Note:

    in the press: in a crowd

•

Don't throw your bones on the floor

Some advice on manners when a child is away from home,
anon., *c.* 1480

> Little children, here ye may lere,
> Much courtesy that is written here.

Look thine hands be washen clean,
That no filth in thy nails be seen.
Take thou no meat till grace be said
And till thou see all things arrayed.
Look, my son, that thou not sit
Till the ruler of the house thee bid.
And at thy meat, in the beginning,
Look on poor men that thou think:
For the full stomach ever fails
To understand what the hungry ails.
Eat not thy meat too hastily,
Abide and eat easily.
Carve not thy bread too thin,
Nor break it not in twain:
The morsels that thou beginnest to touch
Cast them not in thy pouch.
Put not thy fingers in thy dish,
Neither in flesh, neither in fish;
Put not thy meat into the salt
(Into thy cellar that thy salt halt)
But lay it fair on thy trencher
Before thee, that is honour.

Pick not thine ears nor thy nostrils,
If thou do, men will say thou com'st of churls.
And while thy meat in thy mouth is
Drink thou not – forget not this.

Eat thy meat by small morsels,
Fill not thy mouth as doeth rascals.
Pick not thy teeth with thy knife;
In no company begin thou strife.
And when thou hast thy pottage done,
Out of thy dish put thou thy spoon.
Nor spit thou not over the table
Nor thereupon – for it is not able.
Lay not thine elbow nor thy fist
Upon the table whilst thou eat'st.
Bulk not, as a bean were in thy throat,
As a churl that comes out of a cot.
And if thy meat be of great price
Be ware of it, or thou art not wise.

Bite not thy meat, but carve it clean:
Be well ware no drop be seen.
When thou eatest gape not too wide,
That thy mouth be seen on every side.
And son, be ware, I rede, of one thing,
Blow neither in thy meat nor in thy drink.

And cast not thy bones unto the floor,
But lay them fair on thy trencher.
Keep clean thy cloth before all
And sit thou still, whatso befall,
'Till grace be said unto the end,
And till thou have washen with thy friend.
And spit not in thy basin,
My sweet son, that thou washest in;
And arise up soft and still,
And jangle neither with Jack nor Jill,
But take thy leave of thy host lowly,
And thank him with thine heart highly.
Then men will say thereafter
That 'A gentleman was here.'

Notes:

    lere: learn
    halt: holds
    churls: peasants
    able: seemly
    cot: cottage
    rede: advise

•

The horrible English

Italian observer, England, *c.* 1500

The want of affection in the English is strongly manifested towards their children; for after having kept them at home till they arrive at the age of 7 or 9 years at the utmost, they put them out, both males and females, to hard service in the houses of other people, binding them generally for another 7 or 9 years. And these are called apprentices, and during that time they perform all the most menial offices; and few are born who are exempted from this fate, for every one, however rich he may be, sends away his children into the houses of others, whilst he, in return, receives those of strangers into his own. And on inquiring the reason for this severity, they answered that they did it in order that their children might learn better manners. But I, for my part, believe that they do it because they like to enjoy all their comforts themselves, and that they are better served by strangers than they would be by their own children. Besides which the English being great epicures, and very avaricious by nature, indulge in the most delicate fare themselves and give their household the coarsest bread, and beer, and cold meat bakes on Sunday for the week . . . That if they had their own children at home they would be obliged to give them the same food they made use of for themselves. That if the English sent their children away from home to learn virtue and good manners, and took them back again when their apprenticeship was over, they might perhaps be excused; but they never return, for the girls are settled by their patrons, and the boys make the best marriages they can, and assisted by their patrons, not by their father, they also open a house and strive diligently by this means to make some fortune for themselves . . .

•

Home tuition

Remembered by Jerome Cardan, Italy, *c.* 1500

My father, in my earliest childhood, taught me the rudiments of arithmetic, and about that time made me acquainted with the arcana; whence he had come by this learning, I know not. This was about my ninth year. Shortly after, he instructed me in the elements of the astrology of Arabia, meanwhile trying to instil in me some system of memorizing . . . After I was twelve years old he taught me the first six books of Euclid . . . This is the knowledge I was able to acquire and learn without any element-ary schooling, and without a knowledge of the Latin tongue.

•

Dirty bits

Etiquette for schoolboys, from
J. L. Vives, *Dialogues, c.* 1519

'Which is the more shameful part: the part in front or the hole in the arse?' 'Both parts are extremely improper, the behind because of its unpleasantness, and the other part because of lechery and dishonour.'

'The third finger is called the shameful one. Why?' 'The master
has said that he knows the reason, but that he does not want to
give it because it is dirty and unpleasant; however, do not press
the matter, *because it is unseemly for a child of good character to ask
about such unpleasant things.*'

•

Beat him

Advice of Henry IV of France to his son's tutors, 16th century

I wish and command you to whip him every time that he is
obstinate or does something bad . . . I know from experience that
I myself benefitted, for at his age I was much whipped. That is
why I want you to whip him and to make him understand why.

•

I hate scole

Manuscript of *c.* 1530, England

Hay, hay, by this day,
What availeth it me though I say nay?

I wold fain be a clerke,
But yet it is a stronge werke;
The birchen twigges be so sharpe
It makith me have a faint herte.
    What availeth it me though I say nay?

On Monday in the morning when I shall rise,
At six of the clok, it is the gise

To go to scole without avise –
I had lever go twenty mile twise.
   What availeth it me though I say nay?

My master lookith as he were madde:
'Wher hast thou be, thou sory ladde?'
'Milke dukkes my moder badde' –
It was no mervaile though I were sadde.
   What availeth it me though I say nay?

My master pepered my ars with well good spede;
It was worse than finkill sede;
He wold not leve till it did blede –
Miche sorow have he for his dede!
   What availeth it me though I say nay?

I wold my master were a watt,
And my booke a wild catt,
And a brase of grehoundes in his toppe:
I wold be glad for to see that!
   What availeth it me though I say nay?

I wold my master were an hare,
And all his bookes houndes were,
And I myself a joly huntere;
To blow my horn I wold not spare,
For if he were dede I wold not care.
   What availeth it me though I say nay?

Notes:
   clerke: scholar
   strong werke: hard or cruel work
   gise: custom
   without avise: without a second thought
   lever: rather
   milke dukkes my moder badde: my mother told me to milk ducks!
   finkill sede: fennel seed
   watt: hare
   in his toppe: harrying him

Go to work

From an Act of Parliament passed in the reign
of Henry VIII

Children under fourteen years of age, and above five, that live
in idleness and be taken begging, may be put into Service by
the Governors of Cities, Towns, Etc. to Husbandry, or other
Crafts or Labours.

●

No more unfittinge festivals

Henry VIII's Proclamation, 22 July 1542

And whereas heretofore dyvers and many superstitious and
chyldysh observauncies have be used, and yet to this day are
observed and kept, in many and sundry partes of this Realm, as
upon Saint Nicholas, the Holie Innocents, and such like, children
be strangelie decked and apparayled to counterfeit Priests, Bish-
ops, and Women, and to be ledde with songes and dances from
house to house, blessing the people, and gathering of money;
and boyes do singe masse and preache in the pulpitt, with such
other unfittinge and inconvenient usages, rather to the derysyon
than anie true glorie of God, or honour of his sayntes. The
Kynges Majestie wylleth and commaundeth that henceforth all
such superstitious observations be left and clerely extinguished
throwout all this Realme and Dominions.

1545 – First English book on pediatrics (treatment of children's diseases) published

1558 – First recorded doll's house, made for the daughter of Duke Albrecht of Saxony

1657 – First picture book for children 'Orbis Pictus' (The World in Pictures), compiled by Comenius, Moravian bishop and educationalist

1692 – First adaptation for children of Aesop's Fables

1744 – First English book of nursery rhymes, 'Tommy Thumb's Pretty Song Book'

1750 – First toy shops in London

1759 – First English educational board game with dice

1762 – First jigsaw puzzle, showing a map to teach geography

1851 – Montanari Dolls (forerunners of present dolls) shown at the Great Exhibition

1855 – 'Boy's Own Magazine' first published

1865 – First clockwork trains

1897 – Invention of plasticine

Martin Hoyles, *The Politics of Childhood*

A gentle schoolmaster

Lady Jane Grey to Roger Ascham, *c.* 1550, England

One of the greatest benefits that ever God gave me is that He sent me so sharp and severe parents, and so gentle a schoolmaster. For when I am in presence of either father or mother, whether I speak, keep silence, sit, stand, or go, eat, drink, be merry or sad, be sweing, playing, dancing, or doing anything else, I must do it, as it were, in such weight, measure, and number, even so perfectly as God made the world, or else I am so sharply taunted, so cruelly threatened, yea, presently with pinches, nips, and bobs . . . that I think myself in hell till time come that I must go to Mr Elmer; who teacheth me so gently, so pleasantly, with such fair allurements to learning, that I think all the time nothing while I am with him.

•

Bunking off

Roger Ascham, *The Scholemaster, c.* 1560

Divers Scholers of Eaton be runne awaie from the Schole for feare of beating.

•

Child marriage: first night problems

John Bridge v Elizabeth Bridge (born Ramsbotham),
1561, England

. . . the said John wold Eate no meate at supper . . . and whan
hit was bed tyme, the said John did wepe to go home with his
father, he beynge at that tyme at her brothers house. Yet
nevertheles, bie his fathers intreating, and bie the perswasion of
the priest, the said John did comme to bed to this Respondent
far in the night; and there lay still, till in the morning, in suche
sort as this deponent might take unkindnes with hym; for he lay
with his backe toward her all night; and neither then, nor anie
tyme els, had carnall dole with her, nor never after came in her
companie, more than he had never knowne her.

. . . the said John was, at the tyme of the said marriage, above
the age of xiij yeres, and vnder xiiij.

•

Child marriage: four in the bed

Chester, 1562

. . . beynge askid whether he ever lay with her, he answeris, that
'the first night they were maried, they lay both in one bed, but
ij of her sisters lay betwene hym & her';

. . . they were maried under age, . . . not past ix or x yeres
old.

•

Child marriage: too young to agree

Chester, 1564

. . . he saies that he carried the said John in his armes, beinge at
tyme of the said Mariage about iij yeres of age, and spake
somme of the wordes of Matrimonye, that the said John, bie
reason of his younge age, cold not speake hym self, holdinge
him in his armes all the while the wordes of Matrimonie were in
speakinge. And one James Holford carried the said Jane in his
armes, beinge at the said tyme about ij yeres of age, and spake
all, or the most parte of it, the wordes of matrimony for her . . .

•

We hate maths

Verse (anonymous), 1570, England

Multiplication is mie vexation
And Division quite as bad,
The Golden rule is mie stumbling stule,
And Practice makes me mad.

•

The kids aren't worth much

Verse (anonymous), 16th century, England

> Of all the months the first behold,
> January two-faced and cold.
> Because its eyes two ways are cast,
> To face the future and the past.
> Thus the child six summers old
> Is not worth much when all is told.

●

Slippery slope

Choirboys in winter, London, 1595

The St Paul's choristers were 'pissing upon stones in the Churche . . . to slide upon, as uppon ysse'.

●

Wool-sorters useful

Report by Thomas Deloney, *c.* 1600, England

Poor people whom God lightly blessed with most children, did by means of this occupation so order them, that by the time they were come to be six or seven years of age they were able to get their own bread.

●

Cock of the walk

Heroard, Henry IV's physician, recorded the details of
Louis XIII's infancy, here quoted and summarized
by Philippe Ariès, *c*. 1601, France

Louis XIII was not yet one year old: 'He laughed uproariously
when his nanny waggled his cock with her fingers.' An amusing
trick which the child soon copied. Calling a page, 'he shouted
"Hey, there!" and pulled up his robe, showing him his cock.'

He was one year old: 'In high spirits,' notes Heroard, 'he
made everybody kiss his cock.' This amused them all. Similarly
everyone considered his behaviour towards two visitors, a
certain de Bonières and his daughter, highly amusing: 'He
laughed at him, lifted up his robe and showed him his cock, but
even more so to his daughter, for then, holding it and giving
his little laugh, he shook the whole of his body up and down.'
They thought this so funny that the child took care to repeat a
gesture which had been such a success; in the presence of a
'little lady', 'he lifted up his coat, and showed her his cock with
such fervour that he was quite beside himself. He lay on his
back to show it to her.'

When he was just over a year old he was engaged to the
Infanta of Spain; his attendants explained to him what this
meant, and he understood them fairly well. 'They asked him:
"Where is the Infanta's darling?" He put his hand on his
cock.'

During his first three years nobody showed any reluctance
or saw any harm in jokingly touching the child's sexual parts.
'The Marquise [de Verneuil] often put her hand under his
coat; he got his nanny to lay him on her bed where she played
with him, putting her hand under his coat.' Mme de Verneuil
wanted to play with him and took hold of his nipples; he

pushed her away, saying: "Let go, let go, go away." He would not allow the Marquise to touch his nipples, because his nanny had told him: "Monsieur, never let anybody touch your nipples, or your cock, or they will cut it off." He remembered this.' Again: 'When he got up, he would not take his shirt and said: "Not my shirt, I want to give you all some milk from my cock." We held out our hands, and he pretended to give us all some milk, saying: "Pss, pss," and only then agreeing to take his shirt.'

It was a common joke, repeated time and again, to say to him: 'Monsieur, you haven't got a cock.' Then 'he replied: "Hey, here it is!" – laughing and lifting it up with one finger.' These jokes were not limited to the servants, or to brainless youths, or to women of easy virtue such as the King's mistress. The Queen, his mother, made the same sort of joke: 'The Queen, touching his cock, said: "Son, I am holding your spout."' Even more astonishing is this passage: 'He was undressed and Madame too [his sister], and they were placed naked in bed with the King, where they kissed and twittered and gave great amusement to the King. The King asked him: "Son, where is the Infanta's bundle?" He showed it to him, saying: "There is no bone in it, Papa." Then, as it was slightly distended, he added: "There is now, there is sometimes."'

The Court was amused, in fact, to see his first erections: 'Waking up at eight o'clock, he called Mlle Bethouzay and said to her: "Zezai, my cock is like a drawbridge; see how it goes up and down." And he raised it and lowered it.'

By the age of four, 'he was taken to the Queen's apartments, where Mme de Guise showed him the Queen's bed and said to him: "Monsieur, this is where you were made." He replied: "With Mamma?"' 'He asked his nanny's husband: "What is that?" "That," came the reply, "is one of my silk stockings." "And those?" [after the manner of parlour-game questions] "Those are my breeches." "What are they made of?" "Velvet."

"And that?" "That is a cod-piece." "What is inside?" "I don't know, Monsieur." "Why, a cock. Who is it for?" "I don't know, Monsieur." "Why, for Madame Doundoun [his nanny].'"

•

Royal toys

Louis XIII's amusements, France, 1601–8

The list of toys given to the future king of France, Louis XIII, ... in 1601: a hobby-horse, a windmill, a whipping top, a tambourine, soldiers, a cannon, a tennis racket, a ball, clockwork pigeon, scissors, cutting paper, and dolls (male only). At four the future king was practising archery, playing cards, playing racket ball, and joining in such parlor games as fiddle-de-dee, hand-clapping, and hide and seek. At six he played chess, trades, charades, and pantomime. At seven – that transitional age when he would no longer be educated by women – he was forbidden to play with dolls and soldiers, and the skills of riding, hunting, fencing, shooting, and gambling replaced his toys. He continued, however, to play such games as blindman's bluff, I-sit-down, and hide and seek, since they, too, were part of the adult world.

•

Be kynd, Dad

Dorothy Plumpton, *c.* 1600, writing to her father from her stepmother's mother's house, England

... 'to send for me to come home to you, or to send a servant of yours to my lady and to me, and shew now by your fatherly

kyndnesse that I am your child, for I have sent you dyverse
messuages and wryttings and I had never answere againe.
Wherefore yt is thought in this parties by those persones that
list better to say ill than good, that ye have litle favour unto me;
the which error ye may now quench yf yt will like you to be so
good and kynd father unto me. Also I besech you to send me a
fine hatt and some good cloth to make me some kevercheffes.
And thus I besech Jesu to have you in his blessed keeping to his
pleasure and your harts desire and comforth.

•

Beginnings

Childhood of Jean-Jacques Bouchard, *c*. 1601, France

He was scarcely eight years old when he started to clamber up
on little girls ... Instead of sticking little sticks up their
[rectums] as children do, pretending to give each other enemas,
he lustily screwed without knowledge of what he was doing.

•

Girls can

Abilities of the young Lucy Hutchinson,
born 1620, England

By the time I was foure yeares old I read English perfectly, and
having a greate memory, I was carried to sermons; and while I
was very young could remember and repeate them exactly, and
being caress'd, the love of praise tickled me, and made me
attend more heedfully. When I was about 7 yeares of age, I
remember I had att one time 8 tutors in severall quallities,

languages, musick, dancing, writing, and needlework; but my genius was quite averse from all but my booke . . . and every moment I could steale from my play . . . I would steale into some hole or other to read . . . I was so apt that [in Latin] I outstripped my brothers who were at schoole . . . As for my needle I absolutely hated it . . . Play among other children I despis'd.

•

Light blue touch paper . . .

An accident to Marmaduke Rawdon, aged twelve in 1621, York, England, as reported in *The Life*

Marmaduke Rawdon of York 'had a minde to show [a girl he admired] what fine crackinge squibs he could make; so he and three or four boyes more . . . had gott some quantitie of powder, and putt itt in one of the boyes' hatts: Mr Rawdon goinge to give fire to the crackinge squib, itt would not att first goe of; soe Mr Rawdon fell a blowinge of itt, and the boy with the hatt of powder came nere Mr Rawdon to see what was the matter thatt it would not goe of, when, of a sudden, itt went of . . . [He was carried home], his head sweld as big as tow heades, and his eielids seemingly burnt up, to the great griefe of his parents, who presently sent for the most eminent doctors and surgeons of the cittie, who, consultinge togeather, did apply thosse things that were most convenient for him . . . He lay nine dayes blinde without anie sight att all.'

•

Beasts

Report by Wimborne churchwardens, 1629, England

. . . our church and the seats thereof have been beastly abused and profaned by uncivil children.

•

Kindergarten Latin

From the diary of Henry Slingsby, *c.* 1630, England

I also committ'd my Son Thomas [aged 4] into ye charge & Tuition of Mr Cheny whom I intend shall be his schoolmaster, & now he doth begin to teach him his primer; I intend he shall begin to spell, & Read Latin together with his english, & to learn to speak it, more by practise of speaking yn by rule; he could ye last year, before he was 4 years old, tell ye Latin words for the parts of his body & of his cloaths . . . I will make Tryall of this way Teaching my Son Latin, yt is wth out Rule or grammer; & herein I do follow ye Pattern of Michael de Montaigne a frenchman who as he himself saith was so taught Lating, yt he could at 6 years old speak more Latin yn French. But I want yt means wth he had, having those about him yt could speak nothing but Latin; him I do take to be my Pattern herein of educating my son.

•

A holy twelve-year-old

A letter from Samuel Mather, 1638, America

Though I am thus well in body yet I question whether my soul doth prosper as my body doth, for I perceive yet to this very day, little *growth* in grace; and this makes me question whether grace be in my heart or no. I feel also daily great unwillingness to good duties, and the great ruling of sin in my heart; and that God is angry with me and gives me no answers to my prayers; but many times he even throws them down as dust in my face; and he does not grant my continued request for the *spiritual blessing of the softening of my hard heart*. And in all this I could yet take some comfort but that it makes me to wonder what God's *secret decree* concerning me may be: for I doubt whether even God is wont to deny grace and mercy to his chosen (though *uncalled*) when they seek unto him by prayer for it; and therefore, seeing he doth thus deny it to me, I think that the reason of it is most like to be because I belong not unto *the election of grace*. I desire that you would let me have your prayers as I doubt not but I have them, and rest

Your Son, Samuel Mather.

•

Ship 'em off

A bequest for enforced transportation

In 1640 Anthony Adby, a London alderman, left a bequest of money to be used expressly for 'poore Boyes and Girles to be taken up out of the streets of London as Vagrants for the Cloathing and transporting of them to Virginia, New England or any other of the Western Plantations'.

•

Free of reason

The nature of children as seen by
Thomas Hobbes, *The Citizen*, 1642, England

Unless you give children all they ask for, they are peevish and
cry, aye, and strike their parents sometimes; and all this they
have from nature. Yet are they free from guilt, neither may we
properly call them wicked ... because wanting the free use of
reason they are exempted from all duty.

•

Of the boy and the butterfly

A poem by John Bunyan, *c*. 1650

Behold, how eager this our little boy
Is for a butterfly, as if all joy,
All profits, honours, yea, and lasting pleasures,
Were wrapped up in her, or the richest treasures
Found in her would be bundled up together,
When all her all is lighter than a feather.

He halloos, runs, and cries out, 'Here, boys, here!'
Nor doth he brambles or the nettles fear:
He stumbles at the molehills, up he gets,
And runs again, as one bereft of wits;
And all his labour and his large outcry
Is only for a silly butterfly.

Comparison

This little boy an emblem is of those
Whose hearts are wholly at the world's dispose.
The butterfly doth represent to me
The world's best things at best but fading be.
All are but painted nothings and false joys,
Like this poor butterfly to these our boys.

His running through nettles, thorns, and briers,
To gratify his boyish fond desires,
His tumbling over molehills to attain
His end, namely, his butterfly to gain,
Doth plainly show what hazards some men run
To get what will be lost as soon as won.

•

Sparing the rod

From the diaries of J. Erskine, *c*. 1650, Scotland

As to the perverseness of the poor young child, it rarely is unconquerable in a boy so very young, if proper methods be taken. I know the boy had a wantonness, as such of his age use to have, and is more plyable by perswasion than by rough treatment. But Cumming's crabbed peevish temper made him use the last method, and often to beat him severely for trifles, and sometimes when the boy was more in the right than he, till I put a stop to it, and now he says himself the boy does well. Lord be thanked he learns well and would learn better if he had a more painfull and better temper'd master.

•

Four years without thrashing

From anon., *A Rich Closet of Physical Secrets . . .
The Child-Bearer's Cabinet*, 1652, England

From three years of age until the seventh, they are to be
educated gently and kindly, not to be severely reprehended,
chidden, or beaten, for by that means they may be made
throughout their whole life after too timorous, or too much
terrified, astonished, and sotted.

Being yet in their first years, they are not to be compelled to
going [walking], for seeing all their bones are soft as Wax, and
the body fall the heavier, they either become lame or universally
resolved in their feet . . .

In the sixth or seventh year of their age, they are to be sent to
schoole, and committed to the breeding and introduction of
courteous and temperate Schoolmasters, who may not terrifie
them.

Before these yeares they are not to be compelled or forced to
harder labours; otherwise they will not thrive well, but stand at
a stay, and keep little, or become Dwarfes.

•

Girls and dolls

From *Of Government and Obedience* by John Hall
of Richmond, London, 1654

. . . we shall finde girls . . . providing apparel and food for their
Babies [*dolls*], with most high and great indulgence: as supposing
they do hereby as really pleasure and benefit these as their
parents do them.

•

Let's get giddy

From *Of Government and Obedience* by John Hall
of Richmond, London, 1654

... by way of sport [they] ... turn themselves often around,
not only for pride and affection sake, to see who can turn
oftenest, but on purpose also that they may then stand delighted
with those transient and giddy figures and apprehensions which
are then made in their brain.

•

Rudeness

From M. Needham, *A Discourse concerning Schools
and School-Masters*, London, 1663

It must needs pity any Christian heart to see the little dirty
Infantry, which swarms up and down in Alleys and Lanes, with
curses and ribaldry in their mouths, and other ill rude
behaviour.

•

A hoyting girl

I was educated by my mother:
Lady Anne Fanshawe, 1676, England

... with all the advantages that time afforded, both for working
all sorts of fine works with my needle, and learning French,
singing, lute, the virginals, and dancing. Notwithstanding I

learned as well as most did, yet was I wild to that degree, that the hours of my beloved recreation took up too much of my time; for I loved riding, in the first place, running, and all active pastimes: in short, I was that which we graver people call a hoyting girl; but, to be just to myself, I never did mischief to myself or people, nor one immodest word or action in my life, though skipping and activity was my delight . . .

•

Breeching little ffrank

Letter from the grandmother of Francis Guildford,
aged six, to the boy's father (and her son)
Lord Chief Justice North, 10 October 1679, America

Dear Son:

You cannot beleeve the great concerne that was in the whole family here last Wednesday, it being the day that the taylor was to helpe to dress little ffrank in his breeches in order to the making an everyday suit by it. Never had any bride that was to be drest upon her weding night more handes about her, some the legs, some the armes, the taylor butt'ning, and others putting on the sword, and so many lookers on that had I not a ffinger amongst I could not have seen him. When he was quite drest he acted his part as well as any of them for he desired he might goe downe to inquire for the little gentleman that was there the day before in a black coat, and speak to the man to tell the gentleman when he came from school that there was a gallant with very fine clothes and a sword to have waited upon him and would come again upon Sunday next. But this was not all, there was great contrivings while he was dressing who should have the first salute; but he sayd if old Joan had been here, she should, but he gave it to me to quiett them all. They were very fitt, everything, and he looks taller and prettyer than in his coats. Little Charles rejoyced as much as he did for he jumpt all the while about him and took notice of everything. I went to Bury, and bo' everything for another suitt which will be finisht on Saturday so the coats are to be quite left off on Sunday. I consider it is not yett terme time and since you could not have the pleasure of the first sight, I resolved you should have a full relation from

Yo' most aff^nate Mother

A North.

When he was drest he asked Buckle whether muffs were out of fashion because they had not sent him one.

●

The death of Papa

From a recollection by Richard Steele in 1677
from *The Tatler*, 6 June 1710, England

The first sense of sorrow I ever knew was upon the death of my father, at which time I was not quite five years of age; but was rather amazed at what all the house meant, than possessed with a real understanding why nobody was willing to play with me. I remember I went into the room where his body lay, and my mother sat weeping alone by it. I had my battledore in my hand, and fell a-beating the coffin, and calling Papa; for, I know not how, I had some slight idea that he was locked up there. My mother catched me in her arms, and, transported beyond all patience of the silent grief she was before in, she almost smothered me in her embrace; and told me in a flood of tears, 'Papa could not hear me, and would play with me no more, for they were going to put him under ground, whence he could never come to us again.'

●

Sam worried

From the diary of Samuel Sewall, *c.* 1680,
Massachusetts, America

Richard Dumer, a flourishing youth of 9 years old, dies of the
Small Pocks. I tell Sam [aged 11] of it and what need he had to
prepare for Death, and therefore to endeavour really to pray
when he said over the Lord's Prayer: He seem'd not much to
mind, eating an Aple; but when he came to say, Our father, he
burst out into a bitter Cry and when I askt what was the
matter and he could speak, he burst out into a bitter Cry and
said he was afraid he should die. I pray'd with him, and read
Scriptures comforting against death, as, O death where is thy
sting, & c.

•

John, Mary, Betty, Tom and William

Robert Russel in *A Little Book for Children*,
London, *c.* 1696

All the time his Father is a Reading, or at Prayers, he sits
laughing and giggling, and playing with his Brothers and Sisters,
not minding anything that is said. Then another time, his Father
and Mother being in the Shop at work, and leaving him and his
Brothers and Sisters within, charging every one of them to read
their Books; and his Brothers and Sisters being almost as bad as
he, instead of reading their Books they play and rude with each
other: and, oh! there is such a frolic and flutter amongst them as
if none was to be heard but themselves. Then they play so long,

until at last they fall out and quarrel with one another, and call one another all to nought; one is called Dog, another is called Bitch, and another is called Rogue, and another is called Bastard; then it may be they go to fighting, and fling one another down in the House. Then John goes with a Story to his Mother that Mary hit him in the face. Then Mary and Betty go with a story to their Mother that the Boys do nothing but tear them about, and will not let them alone. Then Tom goes with a story to his Mother, saying, Mother, William flung me aground and hurt my Arm. Then William goeth with a story to his Mother, saying Mother, Tom hit me with his Batt. Then Tom crys out, But you lye, I did not touch you, you flung me aground first. But you lye: And you lye: And you lye: and you lye.

The reality is that until fairly modern times most children were either abandoned by their mothers or farmed out to other women shortly after birth.

Anita Schorsch, *Images of Childhood*

Listen, Katy . . .

From the diary of Cotton Mather; a note about four-year-old Katy, 1698, New England, America

I took my little daughter Katy into my Study and then I told my child I am to dye Shortly and shee must, when I am Dead, remember Everything I now said unto her. I set before her the sinful Condition of her Nature, and I charged her to pray in Secret Places every Day. That God for the sake of Jesus Christ

would give her a New Heart. I gave her to understand that
when I am taken from her she must look to meet with more
humbling Afflictions than she does now she has a Tender
Father to provide for her.

•

God doesn't like vain sports

John Gratton, describing himself at the age of ten,
17th century, America

The Lord visited me with the light of his Son, and gave me
to see the vain life and way I lived in being much given to play
amongst rude boys, and took great delight in playing at cards,
and shooting at butts, and ringing of bells . . . I came to see that
vain sports and pleasures were displeasing to the Lord.

•

Nothing fancy at the Wesleys

Susanna Wesley, mother of John Wesley, *c.* 1700

Whatever they had, they were never permitted at those meals to
eat of more than one thing, and of that sparingly enough.
Drinking or eating between meals was never allowed, unless in
case of sickness, which seldom happened. Nor were they suffered
to go into the kitchen to ask anything of the servants when they
were at meat: if it was known they do so, they were certainly
beat, and the servants severely reprimanded.

•

At the temporary store for bodies
in the graveyard

From the diary of Harriet Spencer, aged eleven, *c.* 1700,
after seeing bodies dug up to make room for new ones

. . . Papa says it is foolish and superstitious to be afraid of seeing
dead bodies, so I followed him down a dark narrow steep
staircase that wound round and round a long way, till they
opened a door into a great cavern. It was lit by a lamp hanging
down in the middle, and the friar carried a torch in his hand. At
first I could not see, and when I could I hardly dared look, for
on every side there were horrid black ghastly figures, some
grinning, some pointing at us, or seeming in pain, in all sorts of
postures, and so horrid I could hardly help screaming, and I
thought they all moved. When Papa saw how uncomfortable I
was, he was not angry but very kind, and said I must conquer it
and go and touch one of them, which was very shocking. Their
skin was all dark brown and quite dried up on the bones, and
quite hard and felt like marble.

•

It's my book

Children's 'autograph', early 18th century, America

Steal not this Book for if You Do
The Devil will be after You.

•

Small ad.

Advertisement in *The Tatler*, 9–11 February 1709

A Black Indian Boy, 12 Years of age, fit to wait on a Gentleman, to be disposed of at Denis's Coffee-House in Finch Lane near the Royal Exchange.

•

Alex, Bob and wot I think

Textbook graffito, 1710, England

Alexander Meason can write better nor Robert Barclay, but he is a blockhead at countins.

•

. . . and don't forget the . . .

Shopping list sent by a mother to her husband,
1714, London

Jonny requires the huntssman hunting the Hair; they turn about in a Box and make a noise; and a Barking Doggy too you must bring him.

•

Against quarrelling and fighting

A poem by Isaac Watts, 1715

Let dogs delight to bark and bite,
    For God hath made them so:
Let bears and lions growl and fight,
    For 'tis their nature, too.

But, children, you should never let
    Such angry passions rise:
Your little hands were never made
    To tear each other's eyes.

Let love through all your actions run,
    And all your words be mild:
Live like the blessed Virgin's Son,
    That sweet and lovely child.

His soul was gentle as a lamb;
    And as his nature grew,
He grew in favour both with man,
    And God his Father, too.

Now, Lord of all, he reigns above,
    And from his heavenly throne
He sees what children dwell in love,
    And marks them for his own.

●

Grandpa speaks

A story from Nicolas Restif de la Bretonne, aged four,
France, 1739. It was confirmed by his mother, he says.

'Nicolas, you have many faults, and these grieve your mother.
She is my daughter and has always obliged me; obey me too
and correct these, or I will whip you like a dog which is being
trained ... I want to see you friends with your mother; you
have grieved, deeply grieved her ... Nicolas, your father loves
you; do you love him?' 'Yes, grandpapa!' 'Suppose he were in
danger and to save him it was necessary to put your hand in the
fire, would you do it? Would you put it ... there, if it was
necessary?' 'Yes grandpapa.' 'And for me?' 'For you? ... yes,
yes.' 'And for your mother?' 'For mamma? Both of them, both
of them!' 'We shall see if you are telling the truth, for your
mother is in great need of your little help! If you love her, you
must prove it.' I made no answer; but, putting together all that
had been said, I went to the fireplace and, while they were
making signs to each other, put my right hand into the fire. The
pain drew a deep sigh from me.

•

Grown up

Lord Chesterfield to his son, 1741.
(He wrote many letters like this;
presumably the advice was not taken.)

This is the last letter I shall write to you as a little boy, for to-
morrow you will attain your ninth year; so that for the future, I
shall treat you as a youth. You must now commence a different

course of life, a different course of studies. No more levity. Childish toys and playthings must be thrown aside, and your mind directed to serious objects. What was not unbecoming to a child would be disgraceful to a youth.

•

Dear Mum

Letter to his mother from Frederick Reynolds,
aged about seven, after two days at
Westminster School, London, *c*. 1750

My dear, dear Mother,
If you don't let me come home, I die – I am all over ink, and my fine clothes have been spoilt – I have been tost in a blanket, and seen a ghost.
I remain, my dear, dear mother
Your most dutiful and most
unhappy son,
Freddy

P.S. Remember me to my father.

•

How to be nice

Hugh Blair, *Lectures on Rhetoric, c*. 1750,
on advice to the well-bred youth

Remember that the first rule is never to bring up frivolous matters among great and learned persons, nor difficult subjects among persons who cannot understand them. Do not talk to your company of melancholy things such as sores, infirmities, prisons, trials, war, and death. Do not recount your dreams. Do not give your opinion unless it is asked for. Do not attempt to correct the faults of others, especially as that is the duty of fathers, mothers, and lords. Do not speak before thinking what you intend to say.

•

The drugs solution for children

From *A Treatise on Opium* by George Young, MD, *c*. 1750

... if ... a looseness comes on, four or five drops of liquid *laudanum*, with the absorbent powders, given every night in any convenient form, will seldom fail, unless after eating too much; for an opiate always disagrees with a plentiful meal.

Notes:
    looseness: diarrhoea
    laudanum: opium derivative

•

Dirty books

Memories of Rev. Thomas Scott of school in the 1750s

[My schoolfellows would] often procure the vilest publications; and by the help of indexes and other means ... sometimes become better acquainted with the most indecent passages of the classic authors than with their daily lessons.

•

Dear Dad

A schoolboy's letter, 1752, America

To Mr Cornelius Ten Broeck
                    att Albany.
Stamford, the 13th Day of October, 1752.

Honored Fethar,
        These fiew Lines comes to let you know that I am in a good State of Health and I hope this may find you also. I have found all the things in my trunk but I must have a pare of Schuse. And mama please to send me some Ches Nutts and some Wall Nutts; you please to send me a Slate, and som pensals, and please to send me some smok befe, and for bringing my trunk 3/9, and for a pare of Schuse 9 shillings. You please to send me a pare of indin's Schuse. You please to send me som dride corn. My Duty to Father and Mother and Sister and to all frinds.
                    I am your Dutyfull Son,
                                        John Ten Broeck.

Father forgot to send me my Schuse.

•

Captured

Olaudah Equiano in *c.* 1756 in what is now Eastern Nigeria,
from *The Interesting Narrative of the Life of Olaudah Equiano
or Gustavus Vassa the African*, published 1789

My father, besides many slaves, had a numerous family, of which seven lived to grow up, including myself and sister, who was the only daughter. As I was the youngest of the sons, I became, of course, the greatest favorite with my mother, and was always with her; and she used to take particular pains to form my mind. I was trained up from my earliest years in the art of war: my daily exercise was shooting and throwing javelins, and my mother adorned me with emblems, after the manner of our greatest warriors. In this way I grew up till I had turned the age of eleven, when an end was put to my happiness in the following manner: Generally, when the grown people in the neighborhood were gone far in the fields to labor, the children assembled together in some of the neighboring premises to play; and commonly some of us used to get up a tree to look out for any assailant, or kidnapper, that might come upon us — for they sometimes took those opportunities of our parents' absence, to attack and carry off as many as they could seize. One day as I was watching at the top of a tree in our yard, I saw one of those people come into the yard of our next neighbor but one, to kidnap, there being many stout young people in it. Immediately on this I gave the alarm of the rogue, and he was surrounded by the stoutest of them, who entangled him with cords, so that he could not escape, till some of the grown people came and secured him. But, alas! ere long it was my fate to be thus attacked, and to be carried off, when none of the grown people were nigh. One day, when all our people were gone out to their works as usual, and only I and my dear sister were left to mind the house, two men and a woman got over our walls, and in a moment seized us both, and, without giving us time to cry out, or make resistance, they stopped our mouths, and ran off with us into the nearest wood. Here they tied our hands, and continued to carry us as far as they could, till night came on, when we reached a small house, where the robbers halted for refreshment, and spent the night. We were then unbound, but were unable to take any food; and, being quite overpowered by fatigue and grief, our only relief was some sleep, which allayed our misfortune for a short time.

The next morning we left the house, and continued travelling all the day. For a long time we had kept [to] the woods, but at last we came into a road which I believed I knew. I had now some hopes of being delivered; for we had advanced but a little way before I discovered some people at a distance, on which I began to cry out for their assistance; but my cries had no other effect than to make them tie me faster and stop my mouth, and then they put me into a large sack. They also stopped my sister's mouth, and tied her hands; and in this manner we proceeded till we were out of sight of these people. When we went to rest the following night, they offered us some victuals, but we refused it; and the only comfort we had was in being in one another's arms all that night, and bathing each other with our tears. But alas! we were soon deprived of even the small comfort of weeping together. The next day proved a day of greater sorrow than I had yet experienced; for my sister and I were then separated, while we lay clasped in each other's arms. It was in vain that we besought them not to part us; she was torn from me, and immediately carried away, while I was left in a state of distraction not to be described. I cried and grieved continually; and for several days did not eat anything but what they forced into my mouth. . .

I was soon put down under the decks, and there I received such a salutation in my nostrils as I had never experienced in my life: so that with the loathsomeness of the stench and crying together, I became so sick and low that I was not able to eat, nor had I the least desire to taste anything. I now wished for the last friend, death, to relieve me; but soon, to my grief, two of the white men offered me eatables, and on my refusing to eat, one of them held me fast by the hands and laid me across I think the windlass, and tied my feet while the other flogged me severely. I had never experienced anything of this kind before, and although, not being used to the water, I naturally feared that element the first time I saw it, yet nevertheless could I have got over the nettings I would have jumped over the side, but I could not; and besides, the crew used to watch us very closely who were not chained down to the decks, lest we should leap into the water: and I have seen some of these poor African prisoners most severely cut for attempting to do so, and hourly whipped for not eating. This indeed was often the case with myself. In a little time after, amongst the poor chained men I found some of my own nation, which in a small degree gave ease to my mind. I inquired of these what was to be done with us; they gave me to understand we were to be carried to these white people's country to work for them.

•

Spoilt American kids

Report of an English gentleman returning home
after a visit to America, *Virginia Gazette*, 1767

On my arrival here I found a house full of children, who are *humoured* beyond measure, and indeed absolutely spoiled by the ridiculous indulgence of a fond mother ... Six of the children are permitted to sit at the table, who entirely monopolize the wings of fowls; and the most delicate morsels of every dish ... In the morning, before my friend is up, I generally take a turn upon the gravel walk, where I could wish to enjoy my own thoughts without interruption; but I am here instantly attended by my little tormentors, who follow me backwards and forwards, and play at what they call *Running after the Gentleman*. My whip, which was a present from an old friend, has been lashed to pieces by one of the boys, who is fond of horses; and the handle is turned into a hobby horse ... Once as an amusement for the evenings, we attempted to begin reading *Tom Jones*, but were interrupted, in the second page, by little *Sammy*, who is suffered to whip his top in the parlour ... It is whispered in the family that . . . I cannot *talk to children*.

•

The non-believer

From the diary of James Boswell, *c.* 1770

At night, after we were in bed, Veronica spoke out from her little bed and said, 'I do not believe there is a God'. 'Preserve me', said I, 'my dear, what do you mean?' She answered, 'I have *thinket* it many a time, but did not like to speak of it'. I was confounded and uneasy, and tried her with the simple Argument that without God there would not be all the things we see. It is He who makes the sun shine. Said She, 'It shines only on good days'. Said I: 'God made you'. Said she: 'My Mother bore me.' It was a strange and alarming thing to her Mother and me to hear our little Angel talk thus.

•

All dressed up

Account by Anna Green Winslow, aged twelve, 1771, America

I was dress'd in my yellow coat, my black bib & apron, my pompedore shoes, the cap my aunt Storer sometime since presented me with blue ribbins on it, a very handsome loket in the shape of a hart, the paste pin my Hon'd Papa presented me with in my cap, my new cloak & bonnet on, my pompedore gloves, and I would tell you they all lik'd my dress very much . . . I was dress'd in my yellow coat, black bib and apron, black feathers on my head, my paste comb, all my paste, garnet, marquasett, and jet pins, together with my silver plume, – my loket rings, black coller round my neck, black mitts, 2 or 3 yards of blue ribbin, striped tucker & ruffels & my silk shoes compleated my dress.

•

Trying to be diligent

A letter from John Quincy Adams, aged nine, to his father, President John Adams, America

Braintree, June the 2nd, 1777.

Dear Sir: I love to receive letters very well, much better than I love to write them. I make but a poor figure at composition, my head is much too fickle, my thoughts are running after bird's eggs, play, and trifles till I get vexed with myself. I have but just entered the 3rd vol of Smollett tho' I had design'd to have got it half through by this time. I have determined this week to be more diligent, as Mr. Thaxter will be absent at Court, & I cannot persue my other studies. I have set myself a Stent & determine to read the 3rd Volume Half out. If I can but keep my resolution, I will write again at the end of the week and give a better account of myself. I wish, Sir, you would give me some instructions with regard to my time & advise me how to proportion my Studies & my Play, in writing I will keep them by me & endeavour to follow them. I am, dear Sir, with a present determination of growing better yours. P.S. Sir, if you will be so good as to favour me with a Blank Book, I will transcribe the most remarkable occurrences I meet with in my reading which will serve to fix them upon my mind.

•

The dreamer

School memories of Samuel Taylor Coleridge,
c. 1778, England

At six years old I remember to have read Belisarius, Robinson
Crusoe, and *Philip Quarll*; and then I found the Arabian Nights'
Entertainments, one tale of which (the tale of a man who was
compelled to seek for a pure virgin) made so deep an impression
on me (I had read it in the evening while my mother was
mending stockings), that I was haunted by spectres, whenever I
was in the dark: and I distinctly remember the anxious and
fearful eagerness with which I used to watch the window in
which the books lay, and whenever the sun lay upon them, I
would seize it, carry it by the wall, and bask and read. My father
found out the effect which these books had produced, and
burnt them.

So I became a *dreamer*, and acquired an indisposition to all
bodily activity; and I was fretful, and inordinately passionate,
and as I could not play at anything, and was slothful, I was
despised and hated by the boys; and because I could read and
spell and had, I may truly say, a memory and understanding
forced into almost an unnatural ripeness, I was flattered and
wondered at by all the old women. And so I became very vain,
and despised most of the boys that were at all near my own age,
and before I was eight years old I was a *character*. Sensibility,
imagination, vanity, sloth, and feelings of deep and bitter con-
tempt for all who traversed the orbit of my understanding, were
even then prominent and manifest . . .

•

An old Scots remedy

Memories of Sir Walter Scott, *c.* 1780,
from Lockhart's *Life of Scott*, 1845, Scotland

Among the odd remedies recurred to to aid my lameness, someone had recommended that so often as a sheep was killed for the use of the family, I should be stripped, and swathed up in the skin, warm as it was flayed from the carcase of the animal. In this Tartar-like habiliment I well remember lying upon the floor of the little parlour in the farmhouse, while my grandfather, a venerable old man with white hair, used every excitement to make me try to crawl. I also distinctly remember the late Sir George MacDougal of Makerstoun, father of the present Sir Henry Hay MacDougal, joining in this kindly attempt. He was, God knows how, a relation of ours, and I still recollect him in his old-fashioned military habit (he had been colonel of the Greys), with a small cocked hat, deeply laced, an embroidered scarlet waistcoat, and a light-coloured coat, with milk-white locks tied in a military fashion, kneeling on the ground before me, and dragging his watch along the carpet to induce me to follow it. The benevolent old soldier and the infant wrapped in his sheepskin would have afforded an odd group to uninterested spectators. This must have happened about my third year, for Sir George MacDougal and my grandfather both died shortly after that period . . .

•

The school dungeons

Childhood memories of Charles Lamb in 1782,
from *Christ's Hospital Five and Thirty Years Ago*, England

I was a hypochondriac lad; and the sight of a boy in fetters, upon the day of my first putting on the blue clothes, was not exactly fitted to assuage the natural terrors of initiation. I was of tender years, barely turned of seven; and had only read of such things in books, or seen them but in dreams. I was told he had *run away*. This was the punishment for the first offence. – As a novice I was soon after taken to see the dungeons. These were little, square, Bedlam cells, where a boy could just lie at his length upon straw and a blanket – a mattress, I think, was afterwards substituted – with a peep of light, let in askance, from a prison-orifice at top, barely enough to read by. Here the poor boy was locked in by himself all day, without sight of any but the porter who brought him his bread and water – who *might not speak to him*; – or of the beadle, who came twice a week to call him out to receive his periodical chastisement, which was almost welcome, because it separated him for a brief interval from solitude: – and here he was shut up by himself *of nights*, out of the reach of any sound, to suffer whatever horrors the weak nerves, and superstition incident to his time of life, might subject him to. This was the penalty for the second offence.

•

A home entertainment

A record of the childhood of Robert Southey
(1774-1823), England

As an amusement Southey was allowed to play with his aunt's collection of old play-bills:

'I was encouraged to prick them with a pin; letter by letter; and for want of anything better, became as fond of this employment as women sometimes are of netting . . . I learnt to do it with great precision, pricking the larger types by their outline, so that when they were held up to the window they were bordered with spots of light. The object was to illuminate the whole bill in this manner. I have done it to hundreds; and yet I can well remember the sort of dissatisfied and damping feeling which the sight of one of these bills would give me, a day or two after it had been finished and laid by. It was like an illumination when half the lamps are gone out.'

•

Every man his place in life

A Church Minister's view of education, 1785, England

The children should be taught to read, & be instructed in the plain duties of the Christian Religion with a particular view to their future character as labourers and servants.

•

National order

Report in *The Times*, London, 1788

This day will again bring to the sight of Englishmen one of the most glorious objects of their pride; six thousand children seated like an angelic choir round the dome of St Paul's, with one voice, proclaiming their gratitude to their God and nation, not merely for the clothing of their bodies, but for that which passeth shew, the education and culture of their minds – a sight which foreigners must behold with wonder, but which Englishmen must feel with pride, when they reflect that no nation upon the face of the earth can produce its parallel.

•

The problem with slaves

The strictures of a Virginia judge, 18th century

A slave population exercises the most pernicious influence upon the manners, habits and character of those among whom it exists. Lisping infancy learns the vocabulary of abusive epithets and struts the embryo tyrant in its little domain.

•

Good and bad

From the 'Monitor' or diary of Mary Osgood Sumner,
her lists of 'Black Leaf' (bad deeds) and
'White Leaf' (good deeds). Georgia, 18th century

Black Leaf.

July 8. I left my staise on the bed.
"   9. Misplaced Sister's sash.
"   10. Spoke in haste to my little Sister, spilt the cream on the floor in the closet.
"   12. I left Sister Cynthia's frock on the bed.
"   16. I left the brush on the chair; was not diligent in learning at school.
"   17. I left my fan on the bed.
"   19. I got vexed because Sister was a-going to cut my frock.
"   22. Part of this day I did not improve my time well.
"   30. I was careless and lost my needle.
Aug. 5. I spilt some coffee on the table.

White Leaf.

July 8. I went and said my Cathechism to-day. Came home and wrote down the questions and answers, then dressed and went to the dance, endeavored to behave myself decent.
"   11. I improved my time before breakfast; after breakfast made some biscuits and did all my work before the sun was down.
"   12. I went to meeting and paid good attention to the sermon, came home and wrote down as much of it as I could remember.

" 17.   I did everything before breakfast; endeavored to improve in school; went to the funeral in the afternoon,
attended to what was said, came home and wrote
down as much as I could remember.

" 25.   A part of this day I parsed and endeavored to do
well and a part of it I made some tarts and did some
work and wrote a letter.

" 27.   I did everything this morning same as usual, went to
school and endeavored to be diligent; came home and
washed the butter and assisted in getting coffee.

" 28.   I endeavored to be diligent to-day in my learning,
went from school to sit up with the sick, nursed her
as well as I could.

" 30.   I was pretty diligent at my work to-day and made a
pudding for dinner.

Aug. 1.   I got some peaches for to stew after I was done
washing up the things and got my work and was
midlin Diligent.

"   4.   I did everything before breakfast and after breakfast
got some peaches for Aunt Mell and then got my
work and stuck pretty close to it and at night sat up
with Sister and nursed her as good as I could.

"   8.   I stuck pretty close to my work to-day and did all
that Sister gave me and after I was done I swept out
the house and put the things to rights.

"   9.   I endeavored to improve my time to-day in reading
and attending to what Brother read and most of the
evening I was singing.

•

Dad as a boy

A young lady's account of her father's schooldays
in the late 18th century

Poor John and Richard found themselves in chains. Richard, especially, was always in disgrace, from his unbounded spirits, his exuberant wit, and ingenuity – always a leader of malcontents and adventurers. The boys at Ackworth had to mend their own stockings – to my uncle a most repulsive occupation. In order to extract a little fun out of it, he on one occasion quilted a ball into the calf of the leg, and wore it, attracting attention to it, as if it were a part of his leg.

The awful superior of the school was named Don Bavon (Mary Sewell spelt the name thus) and when a grave misdemeanour had been committed, the delinquent was summoned before the green cloth on a long table, at the head of which sat Don Bavon. I never heard in what the awe of his presence consisted, but there must have been something either in his bearing or his judgements which caused the green cloth to be mentioned with very solemn countenance. One day my father was summoned into his presence for a very heinous offence. He had caught a fly, and had daintily attached a piece of down to its wing and sent it off on its rambles during school-time, which of course excited amusement. The offence was noted with all solemnity in the notebook of the school, having caused considerable disorder. On another occasion my father was summoned before Don Bavon, and was informed that his mother was dead, and that he should communicate the information to his brother, Richard. My father, wishing to do this gently, probably used the master's word and said, 'Richard, we have lost our mother.' 'Well,' said my uncle, 'I suppose they will find her again.' Nothing more passed; probably he had no explanation to give, and my uncle did not, till a long time afterward, realise what had really happened.

•

An educational sandhill

From *Rural Rides* by William Cobbett,
published in England in 1830

. . . we used to go to the top of the hill, which was steeper than the roof of a house; one used to draw his arms out of the sleeves of his smock-frock, and lay himself down with his arms by his sides; and then the others, one at head and the other at feet, sent him rolling down the hill like a barrel or a log of wood. By the time he got to the bottom, his hair, eyes, ears, nose and mouth, were all full of this loose sand; then the others took their turn, and at every roll, there was a monstrous spell of laughter. I had often told my sons of this while they were very little, and I now took one of them to see the spot. But, that was not all. This was the spot where I was receiving my *education*; and this was the sort of education; and I am perfectly satisfied that if I had not received such an education, or something very much like it; that, if I had been brought up a milksop, with a nursery-maid everlastingly at my heels; I should have been at this day as great a fool, as inefficient a mortal, as any of those frivolous idiots that are turned out from Winchester and Westminster School, or from any of those dens of dunces called Colleges and Universities. It is impossible to say how much I owe to that sand-hill; and I went to return it my thanks for the ability which it probably gave me to be one of the greatest terrors, to one of the greatest and most powerful bodies of knaves and fools, that ever were permitted to afflict this or any other country.

•

A vision

A childhood experience of
William Blake, *c*. 1800

At seven years of age I was set to work in the silk mills, where I toiled from five o'clock in the morning till seven at night for the weekly sum of one shilling. This paid for my board and lodging, and rendered me independent of my father, except for the clothes I wore.

There a remarkable circumstance occurred to me. Afraid of being past my hour in the morning, and deceived by a clouded moon, I frequently rose in the night mistaking it for day. At one of these times, I found all was silent in the mill, and I knew that I was too early. As I stood leaning pensively on the parapet of the bridge, I heard the clattering of horses' feet; and, without turning my head, I asked what it was o'clock. No answer being given I turned to look, and I distinctly saw the appearance of a man, riding one horse and leading another, on the mill-wheel. The clock then struck four, and the apparition vanished.

•

Keep your clothes on

From an anonymous manual of household government,
early 19th century, America

A Mother should by no means appear too much undressed in the Presence of her Son; nor a Father in that of his Daughter; for these and many other things, though in themselves innocent . . . give Boys a Boldness which borders on Impudence; and they are apt to wean Girls from some Degree of that Modesty they ought so carefully to preserve.

'. . . a girl of thirteen has been burnt for killing her mistress: and one boy of ten, and another of nine years old, who had killed their companions, have been sentenced to death, and he of ten years actually hanged; because it appeared upon their trials, that the one hid himself, and the other hid the body he had killed, which hiding manifested a consciousness of guilt, and a discretion to discern between good and evil. And there "is" an instance in "our books" where a boy of eight years old was tried at Abingdon for firing two barns: and it appearing that he had malice, revenge, and cunning, he was found guilty, condemned, and hanged accordingly . . .'

In 1817, a boy of fifteen, the leader of a gang, was whipped at the cart's tail out of Frome for stealing money from a shop; later, three of his companions were transported for seven years.

On August 1, 1831, John Amy Bird, who was then under fourteen years of age, with the hangman's rope around his neck on the gallows, 'exclaimed in a firm and loud tone of voice, "Lord, have mercy on us! . . . All the people before me take warning by me".'

Sir William Blackstone in Walter de la Mare, *Early One Morning in the Spring*

Goodbye, little bastard

From a letter from Charles Lamb, writer,
early 19th century

We have had a sick child, who, sleeping or not sleeping, next to
me, with a pasteboard partition between, killed my sleep. The
little bastard is gone.

•

Curing prostitution in the colony

Governor King reports to the Duke of Portland,
Sydney, Australia, 1802

Soon after I arrived here the sight of so many girls between the
age of eight and twelve, verging on that brink of ruin and
prostitution which several had fallen into, induced me to set
about rescuing the elder girls from the snares laid for them, and
which the horrible example and treatment of many of their
parents hurried them into ... Forty-nine girls from seven to
fourteen years old were received into the charge of as eligible
people for that purpose [presumably running the orphanage] as
could be selected in this colony ... The children are taught
needlework, reading, spinning, and some few writing.

•

Keep the clothes decent

From *A Familiar View of the Domestic Education of Children*,
by Dr Christian Augustus Struve, 1802

The dress of children should be different from that of adults. – It is
disgusting to behold a child disfigured by dress, so as to
resemble a monkey rather than a human creature . . . A suitable
dress for young people ought to shew, by the contrast it forms
to that of adults, how far the latter have trespassed upon the
laws of decorum, and how little attention is generally paid to
health and convenience.

•

A less than useful wall

William Hutton, five years old in 1805, from *Life*, 1882

I now went to school to Mr Thomas Meat, who often took
occasion to beat my head against the wall, holding it by the
hair, but could never beat any learning into it; I hated all books
but those of pictures.

•

Scenes of our childhood

Written by the English poet John Clare (1793–1864)
when he was ten years old

O dear to us ever the scenes of our childhood
The green spots we played in the school where we met
The heavy old desk where we thought of the wild-wood
Where we pored o'er the sums which the master had set
I loved the old church-school, both inside and outside
I loved the dear ash trees and sycamore too
The graves where the buttercups burning gold outvied
And the spire where pelitory dangled and grew

The bees i' the wall that were flying about
The thistles, the henbane and mallows all day
And crept in their holes when the sun had gone out
And the butterfly ceased on the blossoms to play
O dear is the round stone upon the green hill
The pinfold hoof printed with oxen – and bare
The old princess-feather tree growing there still
And the swallows and martins wheeling round in the air

Where the chaff whipping outwards lodges round the barn door
And the dunghill cock struts with his hens in the rear
And sings 'Cockadoodle' full twenty times o'er
And then claps his wings as he'd fly in the air
And there's the old cross with its round about steps
And the weathercock creaking quite round in the wind
And there's the old hedge with its glossy red heps
Where the green-linnet's nest I have hurried to find –

– To be in time for the school or before the bell rung.
Here's the odd martin's nest o'er the shoemaker's door
On the shoemaker's chimney the old swallows sung
That had built and sung there in the seasons before

Then we went to seek pootys among the old furze
On the heaths, in the meadows beside the deep lake
And return'd with torn clothes all covered wi' burrs
And oh what a row my fond mother would make

Then to play boiling kettles just by the yard door
Seeking out for short sticks and a bundle of straw
Bits of pots stand for teacups after sweeping the floor
And the children are placed under school-mistress's awe
There's one set for pussy, another for doll
And for butter and bread they'll each nibble an awe
And on a great stone as a table they loll
The finest small tea-party ever you saw

The stiles we rode upon 'all a cock-horse'
The mile a minute swee
On creaking gates – the stools o' moss
What happy seats had we
There's nought can compare to the days of our childhood
The mole-hills like sheep in a pen
Where the clodhopper sings like the bird in the wild wood
All forget us before we are men

Notes:

pelitory: a bushy plant
pinfold: cattle enclosure
heps: rose hips
pootys: young partridges
awe: haw
swee: swing

•

A delightful dawdle

From the diary of Ellen Weeton, *c.* 1807

I have been much diverted with Mary today. I took her by the hand, and she walked all the way from hence as far as our late house in Chapel-lane. She had so many things to look at, that I thought we should scarcely ever arrive. She stopped at every door, to look into the houses. There were many groups of little children in the street, and she would walk up to them, and shout at them; she set her foot upon the step of a door where there happened to be a cake-shop, so I bought her a cake; and then she wanted to stand still in the street whilst she ate it.

•

A little devil

From the diary of Marjory Fleming, aged seven,
in 1810, England

I confess that I have been more like a little young Devil than a creature for when Isabella went up the stairs to teach me religion and multiplication and to be good and all my other lessons I stamped with my feet and threw my new hat which she made on the ground and was sulky an was dreadfully passionate but she never whiped me but gently said Marjory go into another room and think what a great crime you are committing letting your temper git the better of you but I went so sulkely that the Devil got the better of me but she never never whip[s] me so that I think I would be the better of it and the next time that I behave ill I think she should do it for she never does it but she is very indulgent to me.

•

A good teacher

School memories of Mary Sewell, 1882

... a bright young governess ... a fine creature, all life and intelligence ... and our school became a pleasure. She was specially clever in teaching history, and giving it the charm of reality. She would read Roman and Grecian history to us, and then talk about it; then she would make an abstract of what we had read, which we learned by heart and repeated, not like parrots, for I know I had a living appreciation of both characters and events. The coldest day in winter I would sit muffled up in a quiet place to learn the history lesson. She introduced us to a much more stirring kind of poetry than we had known before. In the afternoon whilst we worked she would draw from her own store of imagination and produce little romances. Once a week a French master came from Norwich; also a drawing-master, who taught many families in the county. He was a pleasant, friendly man. He would bait his horse in my father's stable, take tea with us, and then go on to some one else. There is no knowing what we might have turned out had this governess remained to carry us along the way of knowledge in such high heart ... She entirely fulfilled my father's idea of a teacher for children, and great was his sorrow, in watching her successor, Miss Wardell, to see that, instead of climbing, we slid down the hill.

•

Memories and feelings

Three extracts from the autobiography of
Harriet Martineau (1802–76), published in England in 1877

I was carried down a flight of steep back stairs, and Rachel (a
year and half older than I) clung to the nursemaid's gown, and
Elizabeth was going before (still quite a little girl), when I put
down my finger ends to feel a flat velvet button on the top of
Rachel's bonnet. The rapture of the sensation was really monstrous, as I remember it now. Those were our mourning bonnets
for a near relation; and this marks the date, proving me to have
been only two years old.

Sometimes, I was panic struck at the head of the stairs, and
was sure I could never get down; and I could never cross the
yard to the garden without flying and panting and fearing to
look behind, because a wild beast was after me. The starlight
sky was the worst; it was always coming down, to stifle and
crush me, and rest upon my head . . .

It now occurs to me, and it may be worth while to note it,
what the extremest terror of all was about. We were often sent
to walk on the Castle Hill at Norwich. In the wide area below,
the residents were wont to expose their feather-beds, and to
beat them with a stick. That sound – a dull shock – used to
make my heart stand still; and it was no use my standing at the
rails above, and seeing the process. The striking of the blow
and the arrival of the sound did not correspond, and this made
matters worse. I hated that walk; and I believe for that reason.
My parents knew nothing of all this.

One summer morning, I went into the drawing-room, which
was not much used in those days, and saw a sight which made
me hide my face in a chair, and scream with terror. The drops

of the lustres on the mantlepiece, on which the sun was shining, were somehow set in motion, and the prismatic colours danced vehemently on the walls. I thought they were alive – imps of some sort; and I never dared go into that room alone in the morning, from that time forward. I am afraid I must own that my heart has beat, all my life long, at the dancing of prismatic colours on the wall.

•

Busy day

A day at a London elementary school, 1814

Morning
The schools open precisely at nine with prayers, consisting of the 2d and 3rd collects of morning service, the Lord's Prayer, and 'the Grace of our Lord', read by one of the children; and every child not present at prayers, and not assigning a satisfactory reason for absence, is detained after school-hours from five to thirty minutes.

After prayers the first aisle cipher till ten – learn by heart religious exercises till half-past ten – read till eleven – and read till the schools are dismissed, at twelve.

Second aisle write till half-past nine – learn religious exercises till ten – read till eleven – and cipher till twelve.

Third aisle learn religious exercises till half-past nine – and read and write alternately till twelve.

Afternoon
The schools re-open at two. The girls' school, still in classes with teachers, assistants, &c. learn knitting and needle-work till half-past four, and arithmetical tables till five.

The boys' school – first aisle cipher till three – write till half-past three – read till half-past four, – and learn arithmetical tables till five.

Second aisle write till half-past two – read till half-past three – cipher till half-past four, – and learn arithmetical tables till five.

Third aisle read and write till half-past four, and learn arithmetical tables or cipher till five; at which hour both schools are dismissed with the Gloria Patria, sung by the children after prayers read by one of the children.

•

Slave-girl

An account by Elizabeth Keckley of life in Virginia and North Carolina, *c.* 1820, from *Behind the Scenes, or, Thirty Years a Slave, and Four Years in the White House*, 1868

My master, Col. A. Burwell, was somewhat unsettled in his business affairs, and while I was yet an infant he made several removals. While living at Hampton Sidney College, Prince Edward County, Va., Mrs Burwell gave birth to a daughter, a sweet, black-eyed baby, my earliest and fondest pet. To take care of this baby was my first duty. True, I was but a child myself – only four years old – but then I had been raised in a hardy school – had been taught to rely upon myself, and to prepare myself to render assistance to others. The lesson was not a bitter one, for I was too young to indulge in philosophy, and the precepts that I then treasured and practised I believe developed those principles of character which have enabled me to triumph over so many difficulties. Notwithstanding all the wrongs that slavery heaped upon me, I can bless it for one thing – youth's important lesson of self-reliance. The baby was named Elizabeth, and it was pleasant to me to be assigned a duty in connection with it, for the discharge of that duty transferred me from the rude cabin to the household of my master. My simple attire was a short dress and a little white apron.

My old mistress encouraged me in rocking the cradle, by telling me that if I would watch over the baby well, keep the flies out of its face, and not let it cry, I should be its little maid. This was a golden promise, and I required no better inducement for the faithful performance of my task. I began to rock the cradle most industriously, when lo! out pitched little pet on the floor. I instantly cried out, 'Oh! the baby is on the floor;' and, not knowing what to do, I seized the fire-shovel in my perplexity, and was trying to shovel up my tender charge, when my mistress called to me to let the child alone, and then ordered that I be taken out and lashed for my carelessness. The blows were not administered with a light hand, I assure you, and doubtless the severity of the lashing has made me remember the incident so well.

When I was about seven years old I witnessed, for the first time, the sale of a human being. We were living at Prince Edward, in Virginia, and master had just purchased his hogs for the winter, for which he was unable to pay in full. To escape from his embarrassment it was necessary to sell one of the slaves. Little Joe, the son of the cook, was selected as the victim. His mother was ordered to dress him up in his Sunday clothes, and send him to the house. He came in with a bright face, was placed in the scales, and was sold, like the hogs, at so much per pound. His mother was kept in ignorance of the transaction, but her suspicions were aroused. When her son started for Petersburgh in the wagon, the truth began to dawn upon her mind, and she pleaded piteously that her boy should not be taken from her; but master quieted her by telling her that he was simply going to town with the wagon, and would be back in the morning. Morning came, but little Joe did not return to his mother. Morning after morning passed, and the mother went down to the grave without ever seeing her child again. One day she was whipped for grieving for her lost boy.

•

A friendly word of advice

A recollection by Samuel Smiles,
c. 1822, England

I was only an average boy, distinguished for nothing but my love of play . . . I could not have been very bright, for one day, when Hardie [a schoolmaster] was in one of his tyrannical humours, he uttered this terrible prophecy in a loud voice: 'Smiles! You will never be fit for anything but sweeping the streets of your native borough.'

•

Great writer's secret love

Charles Dickens (1812–70)

Little Red Riding Hood was my first love. I felt that if I could have married Little Red Riding Hood, I should have known perfect bliss.

•

Female tasks

Sign in an American orphanage in the 1820s

WHAT EVERY GIRL SHOULD BE ABLE TO DO: To sew. To cook. To mend. To be gentle. To be patient. To value time. To dress neatly. To keep a secret. To be self-reliant. To avoid idleness. To respect old age. To hold her tongue. To keep the house tidy. To make a home happy. To avoid gossiping. To control her temper. To take care of the sick. To sweep away cobwebs. Above all to attend to her religious duties.

•

Making a living

From an unpublished memoir (written 1865) by
Joseph Terry, aged six in *c.* 1822

As mother was much from home, and we had often no fire and no food in the house, I had to seek shelter where I could find it, and procure a little food of any kind where I could. Sometimes scarcely would I taste anything for days together, at other times living entirely on turnips taken from the fields or any kind of wild fruit or roots I could procure. In the winter season my feet, and especially my heels and toes, were much frostbitten, swollen and sore — so much so that after we were in a better circumstance, and my parents could afford to clothe me better, it took years of care, scrubbing and washing to bring my feet into a proper and natural state.

My life at this time was wild indeed, ranging about from place to place, except when I was at what was called the 'Setting Shop' where some part of my time was spent Setting Cards, or inserting the Card Teeth into leaves and Garters as they were called to fit on the Scribbling Machines for Scribbling Wool, etc. This was a most wearisome and dreary task, as we had sometimes as many as sixteen hundred teeth to prick in for one half-penny. Great numbers of children and young and grown-up families got their bread by this unhealthy and poor means; the very best hands never exceeding about one shilling per day, and great numbers suffered much in their health from this, worse than slavish employment.

•

Sufficient possessions

From John Ruskin's *Præterita* (published 1899),
a recollection from *c.* 1825

Nor did I painfully wish, what I was never permitted for an instant to hope, or even imagine, the possession of such things as one saw in toy-shops. I had a bunch of keys to play with, as long as I was capable only of pleasure in what glittered and jingled; as I grew older, I had a cart, and a ball; and when I was five or six years old, two boxes of well-cut wooden bricks [lignum vitæ].

With these modest, but, I still think, entirely sufficient possessions, and being always summarily whipped if I cried, did not do as I was bid, or tumbled on the stairs, I soon attained serene and secure methods of life and motion; and could pass my days contentedly in tracing the squares and comparing the colours of my carpet; examining the knots in the wood of the floor, or counting the bricks in the opposite houses; with rapturous intervals of excitement during the filling of the water-cart, through its leathern pipe, from the dripping iron post at the pavement edge; or the still more admirable proceedings of the turncock, when he turned and turned till a fountain sprang up in the middle of the street. But the carpet, and what patterns I could find in bed-covers, dresses, or wallpapers to be examined, were my chief resources, and my attention to the particulars in these was soon so accurate that, when at three and a half I was taken to have my portrait painted by Mr. Northcote, I had not been ten minutes alone with him before I asked him why there were holes in his carpet.

•

The road-mender's family

Report on Labourers' Wages, 1824

I have a great number of instances of men with no less than ten
children, and the wife, being wholly employed on the turnpike
roads . . . His sons and himself lift the road, the smaller boys
pick the stones, the wife and girls rake the road, and keep it in
order afterwards . . .

•

A heavy punishment

Evidence of Ellen Hootton, aged ten in 1833,
from the Parliamentary Commission inquiry into
the state of children in mines and manufactories

How old are you? – I shall be ten on the 4th August.

How old were you when you began to work in Eccles'
factory [at Wigan]? – I wasn't quite eight. Worked there above
a year.

Were you beaten and scolded at Eccles'? – Yes. Who by? –
William Swanton. What for? – For having my ends down. How
often were you beaten by him? – Twice a week. What with? –
His hands. Did he hurt you much? – No; but it made my head
sore with his hands.

Did Mr Swanton ever tie a weight to you? – Yes, to my back.
What was it tied with, a string? – Yes, it was tied with one
string round my neck, one round my shoulders, and one round
my middle. How heavy was it? – I don't know. It was a great
piece of iron, and two more beside. How big were they? – One
was as big as this book (pointing to the Lords' Report of 1818).

Was it as thick? – No; it was thicker. (Pointing to an unbound octavo book of 419 pages.) As thick as that.

What time of the day was it? – It was after breakfast. How long was it kept on you? – About half an hour. What did you do? – I walked up and down the room. What did you walk up and down the room for? – He made me. Was it that other children might see you with it? – Yes.

Did you ever see such weights tied to other children? – Yes; there was one other that had them tied to his legs. Was there more than one? – Yes, there was two beside him. How long did they wear it? – About an hour. Did they walk up and down the room too? – Yes.

*

Now mind and don't tell a lie; what had you done? – I did nothing but run away because he beat me. Had you stolen any thing? – No. Did you tell your mother of it? – Yes. She said nothing.

Is your father dead? – I have no father.

•

Funny uniform

A letter from Charlotte Yonge, aged eleven,
to her cousin Anne, 1834, England

I went to the theatre whilst I was at Oxford; it is a great large place shaped like a horse shoe; at the flat end sat all the musicians and singers on a stand raised on pillars; in the middle was a great round place called the area, in which all the gentlemen squeezed in if they could; at the tip-top of all the college people all round under them were all the ladies and doctors; there were two great sticking-out boxes like pulpits, at the end of each was an axe tied up in what was meant to look

like the Roman lictors' bundles of rods. The Duke of Wellington
sat on a most beautiful velvet cushion on a carved chair. The
Duke of Cumberland on a velvet and gold chair. His uniform
was very funny; first he wore a red coat, then fastened on his
shoulder a blue coat trimmed with fur; tied to his sword was a
sort of pocket called a sabre-dash.

•

A scientist

Observations by Emily Shore, aged eleven,
1835, England

For two or three days I have observed a species of wasp come
frequently into my room, and enter the keyhole of my dressing-
table drawer, where it stayed a considerable time. This morning
I found two green caterpillars in the lock, each rolled up in a
particular position, and both alive.

It did not occur to me that there was any connection between
their appearance and the visits of the wasp, and I was much
puzzled to account for their being there. Soon after the wasp
returned, bearing, to my surprise, one of these caterpillars
amongst its feet; it carried it into the interior of the lock, and
there spent some time in rolling it up into a ball, so that,
though still alive, it had not the power of moving. I then
discovered that it was the *Odynerus mucarius* or mason-wasp,
which always hoards up caterpillars in its nest for its progeny to
eat; and I was greatly pleased at the opportunity of watching its
curious habits.

•

Guilt

From the autobiography of George Mockford,
aged ten in *c.* 1836

But as I grew older in years, so I did in sin. I was encouraged to
keep rabbits, and any profit I made by them was to be used in
buying my own clothes. My father would have been pleased for
us to buy all our clothes, though he would not have encouraged
me to do what I did to get profit, as I used to steal my master's
turnips and hay to feed my rabbits. At first I was much scared
in doing it, but soon grew bolder by seeing some of the
workmen, who kept rabbits, do the same. In a little while I
could go into my master's garden and orchard, and fill my
pockets with fruit; but I had at times such guilt on my conscience
on account of it, that when I have been out on a dark night, I
have felt as if Satan was upon me, and would surely carry me
off. I vowed and promised to do so no more, but as soon as the
light of day returned, and I got into the company of those who
could curse and swear, and take the name of God in vain, my
resolution melted away like ice before the fire, and I began to
join with those who went to the ale-house, and hear them sing
songs. All I heard and saw there was quite congenial to my
natural heart; I was delighted while in it, but O the guilt and
fear I felt in walking home alone on a dark night after leaving
my companions! I kept repeating part of the Lord's prayer or
some such language to keep the devil (as I thought) from
grasping me; and on reaching my home, I have opened the
door, and getting inside, have suddenly closed it to shut out
the devil. There was no hatred to sin, no sorrow for it; but
the dread of hell and punishment of my sin often made me cry
out, 'Do save me; do pardon me, and I will lead a new life.'

•

A twelve-year-old convict

A Frenchman in the commissariat at Port Arthur, Australia,
cites a convict case, 1839

William Pearson
Arrived at Van Diemen's
Land, May, 1837.

No. 1321, per Frances
Charlotte, tried at Hertford,
17th October, 1836, 7 years.

Trade – Labourer
Height – 4 ft. 8¼ in.
Age – 12 in 1837
Hair – Dark Brown
Complexion – Fresh
Whiskers – None
Visage – Round

Forehead – Medium
Eyebrows – Light Brown
Eyes – Hazel
Nose – Small
Mouth – Medium Width
Chin – Small
Native Place – Nottingham
Remarks – None . . .

Transported for stealing knives, etc. Gaol report – convicted
once before. Hulk report – good. Stated his offence shop breaking,
stealing knives, razors, etc. Tried for stealing a watch, sentence 7
years. About two years ago I was in the Refuge eighteen months
and made my escape. Again in prison about 30 times for stealing
knives and housebreaking, one month; stealing bread, seven days;
vagrancy, two months and fourteen days; stealing money, six
months; stealing money, four months; robbing an orchard, three
days and flogged; for running away from home, discharged;
robbing an orchard, whipped; stealing hens, flogged; stealing
razors, three months; stealing apples, one month; for fighting,
seven days; stealing money, one month; stealing eggs, flogged;
stealing cakes, discharged; stealing fowls, two months; shop
breaking, three months; stealing a gun, six months; stealing cakes,
two months; stealing hats, two months; running away, discharged;
stealing brooches, flogged; stealing fowls, three months.

•

A coal-miner

From evidence of Margaret Leveston, aged six,
East Scotland, 1842, for the Parliamentary Commission
inquiry into the state of children in mines and manufactories

Been down at coal-carrying six weeks; makes ten to fourteen
rakes a day; carries full 56 lbs. of coal in a wooden backit. The
work is na guid; it is so very sair. I work with sister Jesse and
mother; dinna ken the time we gang; it is gai dark.

Notes:

    rakes: journeys
    backit: wooden trough

•

Pranks

A letter from Charles Dodgson (Lewis Carroll), aged twelve,
at boarding school, to his sisters, 1844, England

The boys have played two tricks upon me which were these –
they first proposed to play at 'King of the Cobblers' and asked
if I would be King, to which I agreed. Then they made me sit
down and sat (on the ground) in a circle round me, and told me
to say 'Go to work' which I said, and they immediately began
kicking me and knocking me on all sides. The next game they
proposed was 'Peter, the red lion,' and they made a mark on a
tombstone (for we were playing in the churchyard) and one of
the boys walked with his eyes shut, holding out his finger,
trying to touch the mark; then a little boy came forward to lead
the rest and led a good many very near the mark; at last it was

my turn; they told me to shut my eyes well, and the next minute
I had my finger in the mouth of one of the boys, who had stood
(I believe) before the tombstone with his mouth open.

•

A first memory

Edmund Gosse in *c.* 1852, England

Out of the darkness of my infancy there comes only one flash
of memory. I am seated alone, in my baby-chair, at a dinner
table set for several people. Somebody brings in a leg of
mutton, puts it down close to me, and goes out. I am again
alone, gazing at two low windows, wide open upon a garden.
Suddenly, noiselessly, a large, long animal (obviously a grey-
hound) appears at one window-sill, slips into the room, seizes
the leg of mutton and slips out again. When this happened I
could not yet talk . . .

•

The collector

Edmund Gosse, aged nine, in 1858, England,
from *Father and Son* (published 1907)

I have put away 259 of my shells, 22 of which I wish to
question you about as I do not know what they are.

•

A real sin

Coventry Patmore, *c*. 1860

One of the gravest rebukes ... which I can remember to have received from my father was for my disrespect, when I was about twelve years old, in taking from the bookshelves a thick old Bible in order to enable me to sit more conveniently at my dinner.

•

A treasure island

Robert Louis Stevenson, *c*. 1860, in
Child's Play, Scotland, 1881

When my cousin and I took our porridge of a morning, we had a device to enliven the course of the meal. He ate his with sugar, and explained it to be a country continually buried under snow. I took mine with milk, and explained it to be a country suffering gradual inundation. You can imagine us exchanging bulletins; how here was an island still unsubmerged, here a valley not yet covered with snow; what inventions were made; how his population lived in cabins on perches and travelled on stilts, and how mine was always in boats; how the interest grew furious, as the last corner of safe ground was cut off on all sides and grew smaller every moment; and how, in fine, the food was of altogether secondary importance, and might even have been nauseous, so long as we seasoned it with these dreams.

From 1854 to 1924 an estimated 100,000 children were sent West (of America) on orphan trains, to stay in foster homes and work on farms.

Eileen Simpson, *Orphans*

Backstreet care

'An Orphan Girl, A Street-Seller'

Mother has been dead just a year this month; she took cold at the washing and it went to her chest; she was only bad a fortnight; she suffered great pain, and, poor thing, she used to fret dreadful, as she lay ill, about me, for she knew she was going to leave me. She used to plan how I was to do when she was gone. She made me promise to try to get a place and keep from the streets if I could, for she seemed to dread them so much. When she was gone I was left in the world without a friend. I am quite alone, I have no relation at all, not a soul belonging to me. For three months I went about looking for a place, as long as my money lasted, for mother told me to sell our furniture to keep me and get me clothes. I could have got a place, but nobody would have me without a character, and I knew nobody to give me one. I tried very hard to get one, indeed I did; for I thought of all mother had said to me about going into the streets. At last, when my money was just gone, I met a young woman in the street, and I asked her to tell me where I could get a lodging. She told me to come with her, she would show me a respectable lodging-house for women and girls. I went, and I have been there ever since. The women in the house advised me to take to flower-selling, as I could get nothing else to do. One of the young women took me to market with her, and showed me how to bargain with the salesman for my flowers. At first, when I went out to sell, I felt so ashamed I could not ask anybody to buy of me; and many times went back at night with all my stock, without selling one bunch. The woman at the lodging-house is very good to me; and when I have a bad day she will let my lodging go until I can pay her. She always gives me my dinner, and a good dinner it is, of a Sunday; and she will often give me a breakfast, when she knows I have no money to buy any. She is very kind, indeed, for she knows I am alone. I feel very thankful to her, I am sure, for all her goodness to me.

•

Ducking and diving

'A Mudlark', aged about thirteen,
an Irish boy from Kerry, in London

On one occasion I was swimming a considerable way out in the river when I saw two or three barges near me, and no one in them. I leaped on board of one and went down into the cabin, when some of the Thames' police in a galley rowed up to me. I ran down naked beneath the deck of the barge and closed the hatches, and fastened the staple with a piece of iron lying near, so that they could not get in to take me. They tried to open the hatch, but could not do it. After remaining for half-an-hour I heard the boat move off. On leaving the barge they rowed ashore to get my clothes, but a person on the shore took them away, so that they could not find them. After I saw them proceed a considerable distance up the river I swam ashore and got my clothes again.

One day, about three o'clock in the afternoon, as I was at Young's Dock, I saw a large piece of copper drop down the side of a vessel which was being repaired. On the same evening, as a ship was coming out of the docks, I stripped off my clothes and dived down several feet, seized the sheet of copper and carried it away, swimming by the side of the vessel. As it was dark, I was not observed by the crew nor by any of the men who opened the gates of the dock. I fetched it to the shore, and sold it that night to a marine store dealer.

•

Excuses, excuses

Logbook from a London elementary girls' school

5th January 1863	School opened this morning with very poor attendance in consequence of the wet weather.
24th November 1863	Weather very wet, hardly any children.
8th December 1863	Very wet all day so few in the afternoon that I did not call the names.
11th April 1864	Small attendance in the morning, obliged to give a half holiday in the afternoon in consequence of the demonstration for Garibaldi.
25th May 1864	Small attendance in consequence of the races.
21st November 1864	A good attendance but several children away from sickness and parents being out of occupation.

•

Bug-lore

An American child's experience in the 1860s

We said to the snail: –

> 'Snail, snail, come out of your hole,
> Or else I will beat you as black as a coal.'

We sang to the lady-bug: –

> 'Lady-bug, lady-bug, fly away home;
> Your house is on fire, your children will burn.'

We caught the grasshoppers, and thus exhorted them: –

> 'Grandfather, grandfather gray,
> Give me molasses, or I'll throw you away.'

We believed that earwigs lived for the sole purpose of penetrating our ears, that dragon-flies flew with the sole thought of sewing up our lips – devil's darning-needles we called them. To this day I instinctively cover my mouth at their approach. We used to entrap bumble-bees in the bells of monopetalous flowers such as canterbury-bells, or in the ample folds of the hollyhock, and listen to their indignant scolding and buzzing, and watch them gnaw and push out to freedom. I cannot recall ever being stung in the process.

●

Beloved children

An advertisement in *The Times*, 16 February 1864

Boarding Schools Wanted, in London, for a boy, nine years, and two girls, six and seven years old, requiring firm discipline, having become wild and unruly, through neglect occasioned by family misfortunes. No holyday could be given, as holydays destroy any good effected at school. The father, quite a gentleman, can only pay 20 guineas each. This advertisement is only intended for schools of pre-eminent efficiency for such cases, and prosperous enough to be able and willing to accept such terms, and undertake the needed task of reformation for the sake of the school's own additional credit of success.

•

Eton beating

Account by J. Brinsley-Richards, then aged ten,
in *Seven Years at Eton*, in *c.* 1867, England

As we were all flocking out of school at the end of early lesson, I beheld [Neville] standing ruefully alone among some empty forms. A cry arose behind me: 'Hullo! There's going to be a swishing!' and a general rush was made towards the upper end of the schoolroom.

In the Lower School floggings were public. Several dozens of fellows clambered upon forms and desks to see Neville corrected, and I got a front place. Two fellows deputed to act as 'holders down' stood behind the block, and one of them held a birch of quite alarming size, which he handed to the Lower Master as the latter stepped down from his desk.

[The rod] was nearly five feet long, having three feet of handle and nearly two of bush. As Mr Carter grasped it and poised it in the air, addressing a few words of rebuke to Neville, it appeared a horrible instrument for whipping so small a boy with, Neville was unbracing his nether garments – next moment, when he knelt on the step of the block, and when the Lower Master inflicted upon his person six cuts that sounding like the splashings of so many buckets of water, I turned almost faint.

Between 1870 and 1930, 100,000 children were sent to Canada from Britain.

Gillian Wagner, *Children of the Empire*

A good education

Beatrix Potter (1866–1943), writing in 1940

Thank goodness, my education was neglected; I was never sent to school . . . The reason I am glad I did not go to school – it would have rubbed off some of the originality (if I had not died of shyness or been killed with over pressure.) I fancy I could have been taught anything if I had been caught young; but it was in the days when parents kept governesses, and only boys went to school in most families.

•

Many happy hours

Building blocks are among the most pleasing and instructive toys
ever invented for children. The structures provide many happy
hours for boys and girls, do not readily fall apart, and can be
handled and carried about. Children do not soon become tired
of the blocks, as their ingenuity is constantly been called into
exercise.

•

He learned the boy

A school tale from Charlie Wickett,
in 1889, Cornwall, England

Anyway, this one day I'm sitting at my desk larking about a bit,
and the schoolmaster come up behind me and hit me across the
back with his stick. Well, it takes my breath away, but then I lose
my temper, see. I pick up the book on my desk and start hitting 'n
on the head with it. Now, the old schoolmaster, he trips backwards
over a desk and do knock 'is 'ead on the floor. So I kick him
everywhere now he's down, I hate'n that much. Then I run out the
class and go over the fields . . . When I go home the policeman
and the doctor are there, waiting for me, like. Now, what saved
me was the weals across me back. When father saw they, he didn't
have no more of their talk. He say, 'I learned the boy,' he say, 'to
stick up for himself.' Now after that they said I weren't to go back
to school and I never went for another year. I work with father
instead. Now, you won't believe this, but they got a new schoolmaster and father took me up there to see'n an' they had me back,

and, do you know, I got on lovely with that man in my last year at school.

•

A frightening king

Memories of a Japanese schoolboy, 1890s, Tokyo

The small sanctuary of the Sengen Shrine was built on top of a little hill shaped to resemble Mt. Fuji, and we children amused ourselves by running up and down this miniature sacred mountain. The shrine festival was held on the last day of May and the first of June; and on those two days, snakes made from plaited straw were entwined on cryptomeria branches and sold to the pilgrims who came to pay their respects to 'Mt. Fuji' during the festival.

All my attention, however, was focused on the chapel of Emma, King of the Underworld, next to the Yakushi Hall. This fearsome judge of the dead seemed always to be casting his baleful gaze in my direction. And Granny of course was a ready source of timely warnings: 'Jun-chan, King Emma will pull your little tongue out if he catches you telling lies,' she would explain; or 'Now then – if you don't do as I say, I'll have to tell King Emma . . . And you know what *that* means – out'll come your tongue!' She gave me these warnings so often that, though skeptical at first, I gradually came to feel there must be something in them. According to Granny, the King Emma enshrined in Yotsuya was especially fierce: one day he ate in one gulp a naughty boy who often disobeyed his mother and father. A little strip of the lad's clothing could still be seen dangling from between King Emma's lips in the chapel there. 'It's true, Jun-chan – if you don't believe me, I'll take you there next time and show you, from right up close!' Again my suspicions that all this was just designed to frighten me and keep me in line were quelled by frequent and insistent repetition. It must really have happened, I thought, and tried from then on to avoid going near the Emma Chapel. But the attractions of danger made me venture into the chapel every time I played in the temple grounds, to see whether King Emma really would turn his angry gaze upon me.

•

A silly little girl

From *The Girl's Own Paper*, 28 July 1894, England

STRICT READER OF THE 'G.O.P.' inquires whether a little 'girl of twelve years old may have a lover,' and 'the easiest way to find out whether a boy loves you', and adds, 'I am twelve'. Did this little girl, still wearing a pinafore (if suitably dressed), ever hear of a great dramatist called Shakespeare? We answer her in his words, 'Think yourself a baby', and you will then understand how to behave. Your mother is your best and truest lover, for hers is the most unselfish love that exists. A rag-doll is the best love for such a silly little girl as you seem to be.

•

A punishment

Twentieth-century punishment

The longest serving prisoner in Broadmoor's history was Bill Giles, who died in prison in 1962 aged 87. He was committed at the age of 11 for setting fire to a hayrick.

•

The man's way

An experience recounted by David Garnett in
The Golden Echo, *c*. 1900, England

One morning my uncle came into my bedroom and found me sitting on the chamber-pot. He told me that I must not sit on it because it was unmanly and I was a little boy. Girls and women sat on chamber pots. If I could not stand up and hold the pot in front of me for fear of spilling its contents, I had better kneel down in front to use it.

•

What they say

Children's sayings recorded in 1900

Little Molly, on hearing something that had happened two years ago, remarked, 'Aleck was not in the world then; he was only dust flying about the street.'

A little seven-year-old boy, on hearing for the first time about the Röntgen rays, exclaimed, 'If I were a doctor, I know what I should do. I should turn the Röntgen rays on to a person who was dying, so that I could see his soul going to God.'

A little girl from an orphanage was spending her holidays in the country. She was listening to a wood-pigeon, and inquired, 'Is it singing or crying?'

•

The bedroom

From the unpublished autobiography of Jack Lanigan
(born 1890); experiences at the age of about ten

We lived at No. 1 Thomas Street, off Brewery Street, Salford
(since demolished), two up and one down, no back yard, because it was back-to-back with a large six-seated privy midden – it
was known as a communal midden. The back bedroom, where
Matt and I slept, was immediately over this privy midden, the
bedroom floor also acted as ceiling of this obnoxious structure.
The smell in our bedroom was vile, we had to keep the bedroom
window open summer and winter. There was very little sleep at
weekends on account of the drunks and free-for-all scraps. I cannot remember having any bedding on our bed. The coverings
to cover our little bodies were old coats and sacks, the mattress
was a hard straw one, which was kept in position by long iron
laths. If ever I was invited to the house of a playmate, their
beds were similar. The scene was so common we kids never
gave it another thought. That was our bed, so we laid on it.

•

Family life

From unpublished memoirs of Faith Dorothy Osgerby,
aged about ten in 1900

Babies were not welcomed in our family. I have heard my
mother say on more than one occasion in her middle age that if
she had to live her life again and knew as much as she did then
she wouldn't have had one of us. She told me she even took
gunpowder to get rid of *me*, mixing it to a paste in a soapdish

on her washstand every night. I hope she didn't hold it against me that I refused to budge. When I was born the doctor called me a very strong healthy child, so much so that he used *me* to vaccinate 6 other children from. This seems horrifying nowadays but it was the usual thing then, to take serum from one child to another. Mother even knew the names of some of the 6, who went to school with me.

Well, as I have said none of us had an enthusiastic welcome. I can never remember in all my life being cuddled or kissed or 'loved' as we love our babies today. I think all this gave me an inferiority complex which has lasted all my life. Even today I feel most unwilling to enter a room full of people. I always feel I have no right to be there, and if everyone turns to look at me I wish I could drop through the floor. I always feel even now that I must give place to others. For instance, we were never allowed to sit in either of the two armchairs with cushions which were on each side of the fireplace. One was for Dad and the other for my mother. Of course we *did* sit in them if they were empty, but if Dad or mother came we jumped out very quickly and sat on a hard wooden chair. Well, this must have got into my bones, because *even now* if anyone walks in I immediately vacate my easy chair. I just can't help it. I'm *forced* to do it. Parents were very much above us – people to be obeyed on the instant with no ifs or buts.

•

In 1900 in Britain 30,000 children were at reformatory institutions; 70,000 were at Poor Law institutions, such as barrack schools or workhouses; 70,000 more were at orphanages.

Stephen Humphries, *Hooligans or Rebels?*

Not knowing Noah

At Sunday school, recounted by Ada Cambridge,
in Victoria, Australia, 1903

I myself came upon a crowded class of Sunday-school children
who did not know who Noah was. I was trying to stuff them
with that legend of a submerged world, and I put the question
encouragingly: 'Now, who was the good man whom God
spared when all the rest were drowned?' Rows and rows,
dozens and dozens (they filled that flower-stand-like arrange-
ment of stair-seats running up the wall, which the village school
provides for infant scholars) of blank little faces were interrog-
ated one by one. 'Can't you tell me? Can't *you?*' No, none of
them . . .

•

A warm new sensation

Ethel Mannin in 1906, England;
from *Confessions and Impressions*, 1930

. . . I made no friends at that dreadful little school but I fell in
love with a boy about two years older than myself who had
wetted himself standing on the 'dunce's stool', and burst into
tears when he was finally released to go and do what he had
already done. I felt his suffering terribly and loved him from
that day on. I wanted to tell him not to cry, that it wasn't his
fault, that I understood, that he needn't be ashamed. Actually I
never spoke to him all the time I was there, but I would lie in
bed at night and think of him, and a warm new sensation,
exciting and a little frightening, yet pleasurable, would sweep

over me. He got so much into my imagination that for weeks I would look forward to going to bed so that I could snuggle down into the warmth and dark and secrecy of the bed and indulge the voluptuous pleasure which invariably came with the thought of him. I was six years old and affected by a personality for the first time. I remember that the boy's name was Maurice, that I thought him beautiful with his riot of waving brown hair, and loved him with an aching compassionate love . . .

•

Song

Zulu girls' song

Hlungulu hlungulu goduka	Crow, crow go home.
Amas'omnta wako adliwe	Jackdaw has eaten
Adliwe ngukwababa	Your babe's sour milk.
Kwababa kwababa goduka	Jackdaw, jackdaw go home.
Ubuye ngezotwasa	You will come back
	At the new moon.

•

The tooth-bird

Zulu children's custom

When a child loses his first tooth he is told to go out into the veld and to call out, '*Hloele*, here is my old tooth; give me a new one,' and with that he must throw the tooth into the air. *Hloele* is a small yellow bird.

•

Zulu backslang

Gazaland

A friend of mine was listening to a number of boys in Gazaland
talking together, and at first thought they were talking gibber-
ish; but after some time he discovered that they were talking a
private language, which they made up thus. The language was
Tshindao. The boys cut the words in half and inserted *Tshini*,
Tshino, or *Tshina* between the two syllables. Thus the phrase
'Ask for fire' is, in Tshindao, '*Kumbiro mwoto.*' When the boys
changed this into their slang language it became '*Kumbitshinoro
mwothsinoto.*' The effect is most puzzling when the words are
spoken quickly. The boys practise their secret language when at
work in the veld, and come to speak it as easily as their own
normal language.

•

Australian cowboy

Colin Bingham in northern Queensland, Australia, 1906–7

For years I was haunted in my sleep – and this I would put
down as the first of things long-remembered – by the terrifying
moment when a score of huge steers broke away from a mob in
the valley and appeared, wide-eyed and long-horned, with apoca-
lyptic suddenness on the crest of the rise where the road came
up from the river crossing to the Twenty-Mile. Of all my body,
only my vocal cords were not frozen in terror. With a bare fifty
paces between me and those great dragons, a lithe and dusty
Saint George, swinging a fiery stockwhip from a mettlesome
horse, stormed up the valley and with fierce lashes and fiercer

oaths turned the invaders back to the mob. I was then plucked up by the eldest of my five sisters and held tightly and consolingly against her breast. Young girls in the West developed maternal instincts all the quicker because, with so many of the adult women burdened by anxieties and laborious tasks, daughters so often had to take the place of mothers. It was the same sister against whose side I burrowed in the dark and lonely dead of night when my mother was once away in Richmond, and listened in an agony of surmise to the dingoes howling on the surrounding plain.

•

Kangaroo hunter

'The butcher's daughter', rural Western Australia, *c.* 1907

From when I was about eight, I used to go home from school, put the horse in the spring cart, get the two dogs and go out in the bush, to fetch a couple of kangaroos. The dogs would get the smell up of the kangaroos and want to get out of the cart. I'd let the dogs out and they'd fossick around until they found them, then they'd fight with them till they killed them. They used to bite their throat. If I couldn't follow the dogs, what with the horse, the dogs'd come back to me and then they'd take me to where the kangaroo was. I'd put the dead kangaroo in the cart and we'd go home. Dad used to skin them. We'd peg the skin out and when it was dry, we'd bundle a few up and send'em down to Geraldton to sell them at the skin place. Lots of families there used to eat the meat and we did too. Dad used to take what we didn't use out into the bush next day and burn it.

•

An Edwardian childhood

An interview with Jessie Niblett, *c*. 1908, Bristol, England

When I was twelve my father fell out of work. There weren't no work and my mother was ill. We had no money. If you wanted any help, you had to go in front of the doctor on the Board of Guardians. Then he'd come down and see what furniture you 'ad, an' if you 'ad a good home, you had to sell it. We was having dinner one day, he came, my mother had been to him for help, an' he said, 'You can make that do for twice, what's on that plate.' I always remember that because I went up to my grandfather and started crying, an' told him what this wicked man had said. After that it ran into weeks perhaps with no food, unless somebody send you on an errand and then give 'e a piece of bread and butter. If you had no food, you 'ad to sell yer furniture. If the Guardian man came here today and seen my little home, he'd tell me to sell it.

We had no beds, my father had to sell it all to give us food, and we ended up sleeping on the floor. Then he went to the Board of Guardians and they give him half a crown to buy groceries and two loaves of bread. And that was supposed to feed ten of us and pay rent. And it ended up my mother and father 'ad to go out the workhouse and my brothers and sisters went into the Downend Home for children. My uncle and aunt kept me. I used to go out every Saturday to — (it's called Manor Park now) and see my mother and father . . . I had to go to the lodge gate and say who I wanted, and then the man used to stamp the card I had and I had to go through. Naturally enough, as a kiddy I used to cry when I went in and cry when I come out. The man at the gate told me he wouldn't let me in any more if I cried like that.

Then my mother and my father used to wait for me. My mother used to come in and I remember she had a little white thing on 'er head, little white apron, and all in black. My father, he was six foot and my mother was smaller than me. I can remember the first time I seen them, they didn't bother about me, they caught 'old of one another, they hadn't seen one another for two weeks. 'Cos they used to part 'em when they went in, the men went on one side, the women went the other and they were not allowed to mix. The only time my mother and father did see one another was when I did go out and they used to let 'em both come into the room where I was. They didn't bother about me 'til I called out to 'em, I always remember that.

Then I used to leave my mother and father. I had to go from there to Downend to see my brothers and sisters. I'd be running across the fields. I used to take oranges and apples out to them, that was all they were allowed to have . . . My brothers and sisters, they was alright 'cos they didn't understand too much, see, they thought they was on 'oliday. They enjoyed theirselves. I didn't, I wish I had gone. If I had gone, nothing would have happened to me, what did happen. My uncle raped me, my mother's brother, I was only twelve years old. Supposed to be bringing me up and looking after me. I've never forgot it. My mother laughed at me and my father gave me a good hiding. Said I told lies. But neither of them took me to a policeman or to a doctor. I've never forgotten it and never forgiven it and I never will 'til the day I dies. I was twelve then, now I'm old, I understand the meaning.

I think myself I was the most hated child there was. I've always said that . . . That's why sometimes I think there can't be a God above to allow things like that to 'appen . . . And scripture, oh, it was murder. I didn't like scripture. Instead of going into school at nine o'clock I used to go in at 'alf past. One morning the schoolmaster had me out in front the class. I thought, now what have I done? I thought I was going to get the cane. He said, 'Now then, Jessie, tell us why you don't get to school 'til half past nine. Your mother sent a note with your brothers sayin' you should be

in school by half past eight.' But instead of that I didn't. I said,
'You makes me sick talkin' about Jesus.' He told me I was
wicked an' told me one of these days I should speak me mind too
quick, too much and that the policeman would have me.

•

Is it a dolly?

The humorist Stephen Potter on kindergarten days

Soon we were being signalled for, and I knew what it was – the
form picture. I had forgotten – the midsummer term photograph; and I had been looking forward to it. Perhaps everything
would be all right. There were chairs on the grass – and there of
course was Miss Pegler. I ran up to her as hard as I could go.

Suddenly I was running *back*, even faster, to the cloak-room.
I had forgotten Joseph, the sailor, left in the satchel, and
brought to school specially for this. Everybody was in position,
but with a push and clamber I was up on the chair, standing
next to Miss Pegler.

'Are you sure you want to have him in the photograph?'

What did she mean?

'Well, then, stand behind Kathleen, and don't push, not even
in the slightest.' Did she think, too, that I had been stupid in
the concert? 'I'm not pushing,' I said in a threatening voice.
The photograph was over, and suddenly they were all looking
at me. Monica was pointing at me.

'Why, he's got a dolly,' she was saying, in her fearful voice,
like tin.

'It's NOT.'

'It's a DOLL.'

'It's not – it's a sailor – the largest toy soldier in the world.
It's one of my crew.'

'*It's a doll.*' Some of the others took it up. But I was running and crying at the same time. 'It's not – not – not.' Nobody heard. I got my satchel out of the cloak-room and put Joseph carefully in the bottom. And then I began to run steadily, not crying any more, across the Common, down Nightingale Lane, for home.

•

Out of bondage

Childhood in Hunan, China, *c.* 1910

There were times when I went to greet my father and he would carry me home. In the winter he would wrap me in his fur coat, fearing that I would catch cold. As soon as we entered the house my brothers would give me all the toys they had brought with them, and many of them had been made by themselves, such as little boxes, stuffed sparrows, little boats, and penholders. Then there were glass bottles of blue ink and glass tubes and pipes which they took from the chemical laboratory. The things I liked most were the glass test-tubes. In summer I would catch fireflies to put in them, and in the dark when they moved about, upwards and downwards in the tubes, they looked like golden dragons wriggling and sparkling, and were very lovely indeed.

Father would buy nice things for grandmother to eat, as well as buying me some of a special kind of pretty little buns which had pepper in them. Mother was always afraid that I would give all of them to my playmates, so she always kept them for me, only giving me a few at a time. However, I was not to be outdone by her. Unknown to her I would get some sweets from my grandmother, and then run out of the house and distribute them among my friends.

For this purpose I had to have a big pocket in my coat, and once, finding that one of my coats was not provided with such a pocket, I refused to wear it until one was added. Because I was so obstinate my mother hit me with a stick, and I had to run away. As she had tiny bound feet and could not catch me, she shouted 'Stop!' but instead I ran all the faster, and suddenly I heard her fall down into the water of the rice fields. As it took some time for her to get out of the muddy water, I took the opportunity to run back into the house, asking my elder sister-in-law to save me. Of course she could do nothing, and soon my mother came back, locked me in a dark room and beat me severely with a stick. It was on the night of this occasion that my grandmother told me about my mother and, because I was bruised all over, I slept with my grandmother that night.

My father liked to plant flowers, and in our little garden we had flowers of all colours and at all seasons, and also fruit trees of all kinds, such as oranges, pears, plums, peaches and *pipa*. There were also green bamboos and grey pines. When the roses were in full bloom the garden looked very lovely, and the finches would come there and sing all day long. I spent many happy days in this paradise.

When my father was at home he would always spend his days in the garden, weeding the lawn or watering the plants. At night he would teach us to read classical essays and poems, while my mother and sisters-in-law would be working at the spinning-wheel. Sometimes the gentle sound of the spinning-wheel would linger in harmony with the poems which my father was humming, and it became a kind of intoxicating music to me. On many such occasions I fell asleep in my father's arms, and on the following day when he asked me to recite the poems he had taught me on the previous evening, I could not do so and would say blushingly:

> 'Little Treasure was in father's arms,
> And Little Treasure soon went to sleep.'

'Who taught you to say that poem?' My father looked angry but I knew he was only pretending, and could see a little smile just at the corners of his lips.

'Little-Treasure taught it to herself.' Saying this I flew away like a little sparrow.

When spring came to our village, lovely grass was all over the fields. Red and white flowers bloomed everywhere. Gentle ripples whispered in the streams. The birds began to sing their spring song incessantly. This was just the time for the farmers to plant their rice and for the children to start catching their fish and river prawns. In our part of the country it was always drizzling with rain in the spring, and the farmers wore their palm-leaf waterproofs and worked with bare feet in the rice fields from morning till dark. When I saw people coming home carrying small fish, I knew it was time for me to go out and do the same.

I would act just like the boys, taking off my socks and shoes and going out in the rain with a bamboo-leaf waterproof hat on my head. My playmates were all very naughty boys, and we went wading in the dirty shallow water, trying to catch prawns and fish. Sometimes, when the water in the brooks was running too rapidly to enable us to catch any fish there, the boys would plan to go into the rice fields and steal the farmers' fish, for the breeding of fish is the secondary industry of the farmers in our part of the country. But I did not care so much for fish as I did for prawns and crabs, neither did I want to be a thief. I also liked field snails, but while picking up these things I was often bitten by leeches. Whenever I came home crying because of leech bites my mother would upbraid me very severely, and she had good reason to do so. I would be wet through and covered with mud.

'You know you are a girl, why do you mix with those naughty little brats?'

'Why cannot a girl go out and play in the fields?'

'She just can't. She must stay at home!'

Then I would have a good thrashing, and my mother's angry voice and my howls would fill the house.

•

Orphan Ivy

An interview with Ivy Petherick,
at Muller's Orphanage from 1910, aged nine

It was like a prison, ingraining the routine into you – hygiene,
soap and water and cleanliness, tidiness, all that sort of thing.
I've never been able to get out of the habit. We had to be up
every morning at six o'clock. We all had to file into the wash-
room, and there was the tin bowls filled with cold water and car-
bolic soap. We had to strip to the waist, every morning, summer
and winter, and plunge into this cold water, and there was
this medical lady would stand in the room to see we all did it.
There was no talking. Very few broke the rules, but my sister
did. She broke the rules, talking to one of the girls, and she had
to stand in the passage with her hands on her head, and I think
she had to stand there nearly all day. And sometimes if we did
break a rule, we were put in silence for a fortnight. We weren't
allowed to speak or no one was allowed to speak to us. I was
terrified, you know, even if I heard the trains rumbling by (we
were near Stapleton Road station). I thought the end of the
world had come. That was the sort of effect it had on you . . .
Our meals we had to eat off long white tables, and it was corned
beef, potatoes and cabbage every Monday, every Wednesday
and every Friday, and that was it, the same thing. And we had
porridge for breakfast, and before we could have our porridge,
there was a pulpit in the dining-room and a man used to go up
and read a portion of the Bible and say a prayer, and we were very
hungry. We'd had nothing between five o'clock and the next
morning. Now my sister was difficult. She refused to eat
the porridge, so they lay her on a form and poured it down her
throat, and she spat it at them. She was very wilful, my sister,
and a good thing she was, but in my case I was intimidated. Well,

she wouldn't eat it, but in the end she had to give in because she was hungry.

•

Washday

From an unpublished memoir by Bessie Wallis,
aged six in *c.* 1910

I also hated Monday because this was wash day and the field of operations would daunt the average housewife. All the clothes were first heavily soaked, then rubbed by hand on the rubbing board. This was repeated in fresh water before they were laboriously loaded into the large, copper boiler. From here they went into another tub where they were rinsed twice in perfectly fresh and clear water. The next stage was to fold the wet clothes by hand after they had been blued. White clothes were both blued and starched! They were mangled by hand and when I was home this was my job. It was utterly exhausting work for a little girl but it had to be done. When it rained, black Monday became worse because the clothes had to be dried indoors. Mother would string lines in the sitting room before the great, open black-leaded fire and here they would hang. Luckily, the fire dried them quite swiftly but then came another hated task; ironing. The proceedings on Mondays seemed to go on and on in a soap-suds nightmare which can never be forgotten!

•

Children's strike

Larry Goldstone recounting a revolt of Manchester
schoolchildren, September 1911, in a letter to Stephen Humphries

When I was a lad of ten I used to work after school hours as
a lather boy in my elder brother's barber's shop. Now, the
barber's shop was a real meeting place for men, where they'd
talk about all aspects of life, and sometimes they'd have a big
laugh talking about the school strike that they had in their
school days. I know the genuine story because I used to hear it
from all the different men that were in it. My elder brother was
a very popular young man, real extrovert, and it was him who
was the ringleader of the strike at Southall Street school, along
with two other lads who were brothers. They used to say it
began at first as a mischievous adventure, but deep down they
were very serious about the abolishment of the strap and cane.
You see, the teachers at that time, without any doubt, were
sadists. They ruled with fear. They firmly believed in the adage
that kids were to be seen and not heard. All they needed was the
least excuse – if you were one minute late, if you weren't sitting
upright, or if you had dirty hands, they'd cane you without
mercy. Now when the boys went on strike, they demanded
the abolition of the cane, and they also wanted a shilling a
week to be paid to the monitors, because they were just used as
lackeys. On the big day they met outside the school, over three
hundred of them, and they marched to a field opposite the
gaol walls of Strangeways. Then they marched along the main
road, singing their battle parodies, and threw some stones at
the school windows. The strike lasted for three days, but eventually they gave up and returned to school, and all the classes
were lined up in the main hall to witness the punishment of
the ringleaders as a lesson to them. My brother said they were

held over a desk by their outstretched hands and caned on their bottoms. Now, one of the brothers put a plate inside his trousers, and the blow of the cane broke the plate into pieces, badly cutting the lad's bottom. But they come unstuck with my brother. He was a really big chap and fearless. When it came to his turn, he took the teacher by surprise, wrenched the cane from his grasp and started hitting him with it, then, like lightning, he ran out of the school and home. In the evening, when father came home from work, my brother told him about the canings, and the next morning he went up to the school with him. He was an exceptionally strong man, my father, over six foot tall, and he told the headmaster he didn't approve of the beatings that were carried out at the school, because a lot of the parents were angry when their children told them about the punishments. And he gave the headmaster a strict warning that if anyone dared apply any punishment to his son Jack, then he would go up and mete out far worse to the one responsible. If his lad did anything that required punishment, they were to send a note and he would deal with his son by his own disciplinary methods.

•

She's in the Sally Army

Song of children passing Salvation Army parade
before the First World War

> She's in the Sally Army
> She's safe from sin,
> She'll go to heaven in a corned beef tin.
> Corned beef tin was too small
> So she had to go to hell
> And did never go at all.

•

Sudden death?

Lilian Campbell, Melbourne, Australia,
before the First World War

It was Mass first Friday of the month and if you put a bite of
food in your mouth after midnight you couldn't go to Communion. Sudden Death. I remember that I had to go to Communion
and I'd eaten some green jelly after 12 o'clock and I thought
this is where I'm going to be struck dead for sure. I went up the
aisle to the altar rail, received communion, turned round to
walk back to my seat – nothing happened. I sat in my seat –
nothing happened. I was waiting for death. The Mass was over
and I went out and my dad was waiting with the jinker and
pony. I hopped up into the jinker. Now Dad's jinkers always
went down at the back because the horse was too high in the
front and when it lifted its tail and farted you'd get the full
blast. Being tipped back in the jinker, I did feel sick and the
horse was doing everything that comes naturally and I had to
lean over the back of the jinker and bring up the green jelly.
And I thought – this is IT – DEATH FOR SURE. But I didn't die
and I thought, 'Now . . . ???'

•

The golf links

A poem by Sarah N. Cleghorn, 1915, America

The golf links lie so near the mill
That almost every day
The laboring children can look out
And see the men at play.

•

Dealing with a truant

Interview with Frank Unwin at Highfields Industrial School,
near Liverpool, during the First World War

I hated school so I would sag off, go down the market and do odd
jobs there. Well, when I was ten I sagged off for three weeks, and
the attendance officer he chased me across the market and got
hold of me, and the result was I was sent to this industrial
school for six months. They made you feel like a prisoner, like
you'd committed some great crime. You had to march everywhere; march to your dormitory, march into meals. And most of
the time you weren't allowed to speak; you had to be silent prac-
tically all day – it was to break your will. Well, I couldn't stand
that, because you couldn't stop me talking, so one day we had
a games lesson in a field by the sand dunes and I decided to run
away. They had boys and masters posted as sentries all round the
field, but there was lots of long grass and I managed to crawl away
without being seen. Then I ran all the way down the dunes back to
Liverpool, and I lived rough in the docks for a few days. 'Course, I
got hungry and I decided to come back so I marched back into the
school. I was taken into the gym and the whole school was
assembled. They laid me out on a table and there was a boy at each
corner holding down my arms and legs. Then the headmaster beat
me as hard as he could. I know I was biting my collar; I had it in my
mouth so that I wouldn't show any pain. I wasn't going to cry, and
he hit me all the harder because I didn't. And after that I was
sentenced to another four years stay at the school as a punishment.
In the end I was there longer than anybody else.

Note:

    sag off: play truant

•

Bottom

From an autobiography by Edith Hall, aged seven in 1915

Another walk, after we got off the ferry, would be along the
Thames to Richmond, eventually going on to the common
where I once said, 'There aren't many lavatories for ladies, are
there?' 'Well, we are more lucky now,' mother told my hopping
figure, 'there didn't seem to be any at all when we were young.'
And she said that either ladies didn't go out or ladies didn't
'go'; either was puzzling to me. Once, when I was out with
Rosie I said I wanted to 'go'. 'Well, behind the bushes,' she
said, 'but you mustn't let any boys see your bottom.' I didn't,
but it left me curious as to what would happen if one should
have. The next time we children were taking shelter under our
desks during an air-raid warning I pulled down my navy
bloomers and presented my bum to the small boy who shared
my desk in the infant class. No reaction.

I used to take him broken biscuits and even bread because, as
he told me, he was 'lownced out' at home, an expression used
by children who were allowanced out with bread. He did appear
to be a frail child suffering from the then chronic and common
and not endearing discharge from ears and nose. He wore a
large handkerchief or rag always pinned to his front to enable
him to wipe away these offensive emissions.

On a cold day in the playground he, with four or five other
seven-year-olds, were keeping warm chasing the infant girls
around and when they caught them lifting their dresses. Although
there appeared to be no sexual significance in all this, it just
being one more game, they were all sent to the elderly headmaster
of the 'big boy's' school to be beaten, apparently being considered
too depraved to be punished by a female infant teacher.

●

Absolute silence

Cyril Hayward-Jones at The Mount School for
the Deaf and Blind near Stoke-on-Trent, England, *c.* 1916

There was one side of the building for us blind boys and the
other side was for deaf boys. One of the worst punishments was
to go and live on the deaf side for a couple of days. If we talked
in the dining room or some such little misdemeanour they could
hand out that punishment. That was the only time we ever went
to the deaf side, when we were naughty. Now the thing was, of
course, that the deaf couldn't hear and we couldn't lip read. So
it was a really pretty desperate situation there. Well, what you
had to do was learn to spell on your fingers, to be able to make
yourself understood with the deaf boys, I remember the manual
alphabet even to this day. We used to take the deaf boy's hand
and spell out the words on his hand. Without that we would
have been completely cut off from the world, in absolute
silence.

•

Polio

Alice Maguire, in Norfolk, England, *c.* 1916

When I got polio it was during the First World War. The
doctor thought it was rheumatism, until they noticed my leg
had started to wither away. But they didn't want to know at the
hospital. They were busy with the war so there was no bed for
me. It was my mother who looked after me. She massaged my
legs three times a day until they were a bit stronger. Then she
used to stand behind me with her arms under my armpits and

walk me along the floor. She used to push me to school every day with me sitting on her bike so I wouldn't have to be at home all day. I was learning to walk again but my bad leg wouldn't support me. My great-grandfather was the village blacksmith so mother asked him to make me a special iron support for the leg. It was like a home-made calliper with leather straps to hold it onto my leg. After that I could walk much better. And the kids in our village used to get me to strike sparks on the road with my iron as we walked along to school.

One day one of my friends picked me to do monitor duty with her in our class. But the teacher said to us, in front of all the other children, 'She's not being a monitor, I'd rather see a pin hopping around the room than see her.' She meant because of my bad legs and the way I walked. I went home very upset. Then that evening some of the other mothers and children came round to our house. They'd all heard what the teacher had said to me. Well, next morning, there was a riot at the school! My mum and some of the others went down and complained to the teacher. They shouted at her and really told her what they thought. And she left the school that morning. I don't know where she went. She disappeared for a week and when she came back she completely ignored me, never spoke to me again.

•

An alternative view

An interview with Jim Flowers, Bristol, England, 1918

My father was an ILP [Independent Labour Party] man and he had a large collection of books, Robert Blatchford, Bernard Shaw, H. G. Wells. It was like a university. Well, I was only twelve years old and I read *The Rights of Man*, Tom Paine. And he said that the Bible was like a millstone round the world's neck, and he exposed all the inconsistencies and the inaccuracies in the Bible. He said there was no need for this bloodthirsty God they worshipped. His hands were covered in blood and all this. Well, he blew the gaff, as far as I was concerned, about religion. And I used to go down to the socialist Sunday school, and that put me off going to church and Sunday school and Band of Hope as well. I wasn't too fond of that at all.

•

The Brownies

From the handbook for Guides written by
Sir Robert Baden-Powell, KCB, KCVO, LLD,
founder of the Scout movement

You promise as a Brownie to do your duty to God and the King. That means that you will be loyal to him.

1. *To God.* – To be loyal to God means never to forget God, but to remember Him in everything that you do. If you never forget Him you will never do anything wrong. If, when you are doing something wrong, you remember God, you will stop doing it.

You are taught to say grace before dinner, and to return thanks to God after it. Well, I think you ought to do the same after anything that you have enjoyed, whether it is your dinner, or a good game, or a jolly day. God has given you the pleasure, so you ought to thank Him for it, just as you would thank any person who gave you something that you liked. God has been good to you, it is your business to do something for God in return; that is your duty to God.

2. *To the King.* – In the Brownie Pack every Brownie obeys the wishes of the Leader. So it is in our nation. The British people

are a very big pack, but they have their one chief, His Majesty the King. So long as they look up to him, and obey him, their work will be successful like that of an army in a battle, or of the team in a football match, where all obey their captain.

If everybody started to play the game in his own way, there would be no rules, and there could be no success. But if we 'play the game,' and buck up as the King directs, our country will always be successful.

And in the same way, as a Brownie you must obey the leader of your pack or six.

THE BROWNIES' SMILE.

Brownies always smile, and if they are in difficulty, in pain, in trouble, or in danger, they don't cry, they just

GRIN AND BEAR IT.

That is what our soldiers and sailors do at the Front, so I am sure a Brownie can do it.

Not long ago, a very young boy, named Francis Palmer, belonging to the Wolf Cubs of the 18th Bristol Troop, was knocked down by a motor-car, his left leg broken in two places, and the side of his face badly cut about.

The boy was naturally in great pain; but, to the astonishment of the doctors and nurses, never cried or complained. One of the doctors asked him why he was so brave, and his answer was:

'I am a Wolf Cub, and so must not cry.'

A Brownie can be just as brave as a Wolf Cub: so whenever you break your leg just smile if you can. If you cannot – well – then grin!

●

Finding out about steam

Dorothy Scannell (Dolly Chegwidden), *c.* 1920, London

When my younger sister Marjorie was old enough to be my friend one of our favourite adventure places was Harrow Lane Station, down a steep slope off the High Street. We would chase down the cobble-stoned slope up the iron stairs to the wooden footbridge and feel all lovely and swaying as we peeped through the chinks in the wooden slats of the bridge at the trains passing beneath. When a train drew into the station then the exciting part would begin, for when the train began to start again it would get up loads of lovely steam which would shroud our part of the bridge. We would get into the steam and let it envelop us all over our legs and over our faces and then we would dash to the other side to catch the last of the steam before the train got up speed. We didn't know that Father had seen us in our Turkish bath one day and when we arrived home he shouted, 'That steam from the engines down Harrow Lane is no good for young girls. Your mother should keep you away, the firemen piddle on the coal because they can't get out of the cab. It's piddled steam, firemen's piddled steam you've been playing in.'

•

Afraid of passing exams

Interview with Sam Emberey, near Yeovil,
England, 1920s

There was a fund that was laid down by some rich Lord of the Manor in the area. This was left, this lump sum, so that the best boy of eleven years of age each year could go to the County School in Yeovil and I was mad keen to go. The only reason I wanted to go really was the fact that they had a football team there and I was football-mad, you see. I didn't want to go for academic reasons. And I was telling mum all about this, saying, 'Oh, I can be in the team, might even be captain,' and she said, 'All I hope is that you don't win it.' And I looked at her in surprise and I said, 'Why on earth not?' She said, 'Well, they only pay for you to go there. We've still got to clothe you and get all your uniform and books.' And my father was out of work. He was out of work altogether twelve years during the Depression, and although I was only young, I realized that what she said was true because we went through such hard times then, with my mum working and taking in washing and doing sewing – she was a great needlewoman – and going out scrubbing, doing a bit of charring here and there. We'd never have survived. I mean, she used to make our shirts, dresses for my sister and things like this. It was only on her work that we survived because dad couldn't get no work because there was no work to be had and he used to go busking in the street because he was a musician . . . As I said, I wanted to go to this high school but when I realized the futility of that and how poor we were, then, of course, I wanted to go out to work and though I only had one pound eight shilling a week, that was a great help . . . So I made up my mind that I wasn't going to pass the exam and I didn't either. Teacher called me out afterward and said, 'What have you done with your mathematics paper?' And I said, 'Nothing.' She said, 'No, I can see that.' She said, 'Well, why not? You could do any one of them on there.' And I wouldn't tell her. She never knew why I didn't do anything on that paper. I was afraid to do them in case I passed, so I just fiddled a few figures down and left them all unfinished, you know, so of course I got nought.

•

The hiring fair

Interview with Rose McCullach, aged thirteen,
Strabane, Ireland, in 1922

We didn't go to bed the night before we were to be hired. My
mother got my clothes together. I didn't have much – just the
red petticoat we wore and a vest or two made from bleached
flour bags. There would be a lot of us going together, maybe
thirty or so children from roundabout – children as young as
eleven. We met up on the road about two in the morning and
we all walked together in our bare feet. The boys whistled and
sang while we went, not realizing what was in front of them.
We walked for six hours till we got to the little station and then
stopped to put on our boots (they were big heavy boots with
iron soles). We got on the train and there were lots of farmers
there at the other end to look us over, and we were walked up
to where the big clock was in the centre of the fair. The farmers
would come up and say, 'Are they fit and strong?' to your
mother and 'What do you want for her?' and they'd haggle over
the price. Then the farmer took your bundle of clothes to show
you were hired and the deal would be clinched with a big bun
and a mug of cocoa. And you wouldn't see mother again for six
months.

•

On an Aboriginal penal settlement

Experiences of Marnie Kennedy, Palm Island, Australia,
in the 1920s, from *Born a Half-Caste*

Sunday was church. We went three times a day. Lord, we must
have been wicked people. Whoever sent us there thought we
needed a good clean-out: inside and out . . .

To say 'damn' or 'bum' was swearing. If caught smoking, we
were made to smoke a full tin of tobacco. By the end we would
be so sick, but it never stopped us. If a girl stole money from
another no meals were given until she owned up. Then she
would be punished and then the girls would give her a good
bashing. We were not allowed to talk or mix with boys. They
had their own dormitory. Our dormitory had wire netting all
around and doors with huge padlocks. Girls who got caught
sneaking out would be severely punished. They had their hair
shaved, were put in jail for two weeks on bread and water,
made to wear bag shirts and pants and parade the main street,
white-wash the stones, and crack bags of beans at night in jail.
If a girl got pregnant, well, to us kids she was getting fat. We
had no sex talks and didn't know where babies came from or
how they were made. The big girls didn't know much either. I
guess we found out all at once. If any of us kids saw the big
girls sneaking out we were warned not to tell or be bashed if we
did.

●

A Maori girl's first day at school

Mihi Edwards, aged six, in New Zealand, 1924

All the kids by now had stopped crying. We all settled down and waited for whatever there was to come. Our teacher was tall and looked like a horse, that's how she appeared to me. Oh crumbs, there wasn't anything very nice about her. She looked a real condescending-looking sort of person, as though she didn't like us. Maybe that was just me, looking at her.

Then, a nightmare began for us Māori kids. No more speaking te Māori korēro! We all had to speak English. Auē me pēhea rā tā tātou korēro. Our old people did not speak any other language but Maori to us. We knew a few words in Pākehā the white children taught us, but not enough.

So we begin. The teacher has some pictures on the wall. One is a ngeru.

'C, c, c, c,' and she says to us, 'Say, c, c, c.' She points to the cat and says, 'Cat.' She looks at me and I say, 'Kāo! He ngeru.'

'No,' she shakes her head. She keeps looking at me. 'Ngeru,' I say again. I keep saying 'ngeru'. In the end she picks up the strap and whacks me around the legs. I think to myself, 'I must keep quiet and just listen to her.'

•

Sex education

Interview with Connie Denby, Sheffield, England, in the 1920s

Menstruation started when I was ten years old. I had never even heard of it. My mother just said it was something women had to put up with and I got a verbal rocket for starting at ten instead of fourteen, which was the normal time. I was forbidden to speak about it, even to my young friends, and especially not to boys. I had to keep away from boys when like that, and hadn't to get my feet wet. I would die if I trod on cool linoleum! And that was my sex education! I'd been told that my mother's midwife had a cupboard full of babies and, as I was the bonniest, my mother picked me!

●

Why?

Questions . . ., 1927

Girl (2,4): Where is tomorrow today?

Boy (2,6): Who turned the tap on for all this water? (sea)

Boy (3,7): Who does the moon belong to?

Boy (4.0): Did baby go to the barber and have his hair cut before he came?

Girl (4.0): He won't die will he, 'cos he's a clergyman?

Girl (4.0): Can the sun swim?

Boy (4.9): Why doesn't God make a turn-table, so we can turn back into babies when we are getting too big?

●

More whys

Factual 'why' questions, recorded by
Susan Isaacs, a child psychologist, 1930

3;7   Why can I put my hand through water and not through soap?

3;7 Why do ponies not grow big like other horses?

3;9 Why are the snails in the water?

3;11 Where do flies sleep at night?

3;11 Why won't it (old gas fire) burn?

4;0 (Seeing word PULL on lavatory Pull), Why are there two
l's? We don't need two, do we? One would do, wouldn't
it? Why has it got PULL? We know what to do, don't
we? We don't need that, do we?

4;1 Why is there no shadow when there is no light?

4;5 Why does the water spread out flat (in the bath)? Why
won't it keep up in the middle?

4;5 Why am I not in two all the way up?

5;0 Why does water go out of the way when anything goes in?

6;6 Why do the angels never fall down to earth when there is
no floor to heaven?

7;0 Why can't you see the messages on the telegraph wires?

•

In New Guinea

The preoccupations of young people, 1930

When they were tired they gathered in groups and sang long
monotonous songs over and over:

> I am a man,
> I have no wife.
> I am a man, I have no wife.
> I will get a wife in Bunei
> From my father's cross-cousins,
> From my father's cross-cousins.
> I am a man,
> I am a man,
> I have no wife –

Or they made string figures, or burnt decorative scars on each other's arms with red-hot twigs.

Conversation turned on who was oldest, who tallest, who had the most burned beauty spots, whether Nane caught a turtle yesterday or today, when the canoe would be back from Mok, what a big fight Sanau and Kemai had over that pig, how frightening a time Pomasa had on the shipwrecked canoe. When they do discuss events of adult life it is in very practical terms. So Kawa, aged four, remarked, 'Kilipak, give me some paper.' 'What do you want it for?' 'To make cigarettes.' 'But where's the tobacco coming from?' 'Oh, the death feast.' 'Whose?' 'Alupu's.' 'But she's not dead yet.' 'No, but she soon will be.'

Argumentative conversations sometimes ending in fisticuffs were very common. They had an enormous passion for accuracy, a passion in which they imitated their elders, who would keep the village awake all night over an argument as to whether a child, dead ten years, had been younger or older than some person still living.

On a shaded veranda a group of children are playing cat's cradle.

'Molung is going to die,' remarks one little girl, looking up from her half-completed string figure.

'Who says so?' demands a small boy, leaning over to light his cigarette at a glowing bit of wood which lies on the floor.

'My mother. Molung has a snake in her belly.'

The other children pay no attention to this announcement, but one four-year-old adds after a moment's reflexion, 'She had a baby in her belly.'

'Yes, but the baby came out. It lives in the back of our house. My grandmother looks out for it.'

'If Molung dies, you can keep the baby,' says the small boy. 'Listen!'

From the house across the water a high piercing wail of many voices sounds, all crying in chorus, 'My mother, my mother, my mother, oh, what can be the matter?'

'Is she dead yet?' asks the small boy, wriggling to the edge of the veranda. Nobody answers him. 'Look.' From the rear of the house of illness, a large canoe slides away, laden high with cooking-pots. An old woman, gaunt of face, and with head uncovered in her haste, punts the canoe along the waterway.

'That's Ndrantche, the mother of Molung,' remarks the first little girl.

'Look, there goes Ndrantche with a canoe full of pots,' shout the children.

Two women come to the door of the house and look out. 'Oho,' says one. 'She's getting the pots away so that when all the mourners come, the pots won't be broken.'

'When will Molung die?' asks little Itong, and 'Come for a swim,' she adds, diving off the veranda without waiting for an answer.

•

Never for killing's sake

Kath Walker (Oodgeroo Noonuccal),
Stradbroke Island, Queensland, Australia, *c.* 1930

One day we five older children, two boys and three girls, decided to follow the noise of the blueys and greenies screeching from the flowering gums. We armed ourselves with our slingshots and made our way towards the trees.

My sisters and I always shot at our quarry from the ground. The boys would climb onto the branches of the gum-trees, stand quite still, and pick out the choicest and healthiest birds in the flock. My elder brother was by far the best shot of all of us.

He was always boasting about, it, too. But never in front of our mother and father, because he would have been punished for his vanity. He only boasted in front of us, knowing that we wouldn't complain about him to our parents.

The boys ordered us to take up our positions under the trees as quietly as possible. 'Don't make so much noise!' they told us. In spite of the disgust we felt for our boastful brother, we always let him start the shooting. He was a dead shot, and we all knew it. Now we watched as he drew a bead on the large bluey straight across from him. The bird seemed intent on its honey-gathering from the gum-tree. We held our breath and our brother fired.

Suddenly there was a screeching from the birds and away they flew, leaving my brother as astonished as we were ourselves. He had been so close to his victim that it seemed impossible he should have missed . . . but he had. We looked at him, and his face of blank disbelief was just too much for us. We roared with laughter. My other brother jumped to the ground and rolled over and over, laughing his head off. But the more we laughed, the angrier my elder brother became.

Then, seeming to join in the fun, a kookaburra in a nearby tree started his raucous chuckle, which rose to full pitch just as though he, too, saw the joke.

In anger my elder brother brought up his sling-shot and fired blindly at the sound. 'Laugh at me, would you!' he called out. He hadn't even taken time to aim.

Our laughter was cut short by the fall of the kookaburra to the ground. My brother, horrified, his anger gone, climbed down and we gathered silently around the stricken bird. That wild aim had broken the bird's wing beyond repair. We looked at each other in frightened silence, knowing full well what we had done. We had broken that strict rule of the Aboriginal law. We had killed for the sake of killing – and we had destroyed a bird we were forbidden to destroy. The Aborigine does not eat the kookaburra. His merry laughter is allowed to go unchecked, for he brings happiness to the tribes. We call him our brother and friend.

We did not see our father coming towards us. He must have been looking for firewood. When he came upon us, we parted to allow him to see what had happened. He checked his anger by remaining silent and picking up a fallen branch. Mercifully he put the stricken bird out of its misery. Then he ordered us home.

On the way back we talked with awesome foreboding of the punishment we knew would come. I wished our father would beat us, but we all knew it would not be a quick punishment. Besides, Dad never beat us. No, we knew the punishment would be carefully weighed to fit the crime. When we got home, our mother was told to give us our meal. Nothing was said of the dead kookaburra, but we knew Dad would broach the subject after we had eaten. None of us felt hungry, and our mother only played with her food. We knew that Dad had decided upon the punishment, and that Mother had agreed to it, even if she felt unhappy about it.

It was our mother who ordered us to bring into the backyard our bandicoot traps, our sling-shots, and every other weapon we had. We had to place them in a heap in the yard, while our father carefully checked every item. Our big black dog stood with us. He always did that when there was trouble in the family. Although he could not possibly understand the ways of human beings, he could nevertheless interpret an atmosphere of trouble when it came.

Father spoke for the first time since we had killed the kookaburra. He asked for no excuses for what we had done, and we did not offer any. We must all take the blame. That is the way of the Aborigine. Since we had killed for the sake of killing, the punishment was that for three months we should not hunt or use our weapons. For three months we would eat only the white man's hated rations.

During those three months our stomachs growled, and our puzzled dog would question with his eyes and wagging tail why we sat around wasting our time when there was hunting to be done.

It happened a long time ago. Yet in my dreams, the sad, suffering eyes of the kookaburra, our brother and friend, still haunt me.

•

Late again, boy

From an interview with Bill Bees,
Gloucestershire, England, 1930s

And I used to 'ave to get up every mornin' to go to this slag heap 'cos we couldn't afford to buy coal, an' on this slag heap you could 'ave it for nothin'. I've been many a time with no shoes or socks on, an' going to there you 'ad to go through a mucky yard, an' if it'd been raining, the water'd hang in there, but my feet was 'ardenened to it – my feet was as hard as nails. Used to walk through this water, didn't bother to wipe 'em or anythin', and when you finished gettin' out of the water, you just shake yer feet an' they'd dry. But when it'd been snowing I used to walk behind me father in his footsteps, because where he did work he did 'ave to pass the colliery. I did step in his boot marks. But where he walked out, he did take such big steps that I did sometimes miss an' go in the snow. An' he did say, 'You follow me, son, you'll be alright.' And that's what they call followin' in yer father's footsteps. [Laughter] But those mornings it didn't make no difference if I came 'ome wet through; I still 'ad to go to school after. It was like a quick lick and a promise. 'Where's the towel, mother?' an' no grub, then run to school. No breakfast, never 'eard of that in my day.

When you got to school you knew what you was going to get. You was going to get the cane for being late. If I wasn't in when the handbell went at nine o'clock, the doors would be bolted so you couldn't sneak in after roll call. You was left then to explain why you were so late. I had to tell 'im what I 'ad to do for my mother but he didn't believe me and he would get the cane out and give me three good smashings across my hand.

•

Cursed

David Swift, born with an hereditary muscular disease,
Nottingham, England, 1930s

My grandma used to say that I'd been cursed and that I was being punished by God for what I'd done in a past life. That was why I was disabled she said, and when I'd served out this punishment everything would be all right. I used to wonder what it was I'd done so bad to make me like this. I felt as if, well, if I'm cursed I ought to be aware of why, didn't I? But I had no idea what it could be. Nobody seemed to care. Perhaps my mum and dad were trying to cope with their own lives, I don't know. But they never showed me any affection. I couldn't speak about my feelings because weakness wasn't tolerated. My dad made me hard, hard inside. He was always wanting me to be tough. He never showed me any sympathy and I never felt like there was any love for me there. I felt as though I were different, like a freak in a side show. I remember when we all used to go to Nottingham Goose Fair and they used to have side shows and all the freaks would lay there. And I always remember thinking to myself. I wonder if I should sit up there with my feet showing? You know and people pay sixpence a time, coming in and looking at my feet. There was nobody else around like me was there? There was nowhere else I could go. I used to have this great fear that they would get rid of me or put me down because I was disabled. Fathers used to take cats and drown them in the river and I used to think that's the way they would do it to me, that's the way they killed you. We had a dog called Pete and he broke his leg. So they decided to have him destroyed and I used to think, well, why destroy dogs that can walk on three legs? I thought, perhaps they put human beings down as well, perhaps they'll destroy me, because I can't walk? I used to spend a lot of time on my own in the graveyard. I used to ponder over all the things that you saw on the grave-stones you know. I used to think, I wonder if God needs me more than they, I wonder if God's wanting me? I didn't want God to want me, I was too young. I wanted to stay on this earth. I had this constant fear that they were going to get me. I didn't want to die.

•

Bloody Jew

Zelda D'Aprano, Melbourne, Australia, in the 1930s

When we were of pre-school age, mum would tie a cord around the iron gate to prevent us from running onto the road. The verandah then became a cage where Leon and I peered through the iron bars at the passing parade. Several older children walked past on their way to the shop, and as they did so, they observed us peering at them, 'Jew, Jew, you bloody Jew' they yelled. We were too young to know what Jews were, but the manner in which this was said made me, being two years older than Leon, aware that we were being attacked. When the children were returning from the shop, mum was approaching the verandah when she heard me yell: 'Jew, Jew, you're a bloody Jew'.

We were at a friend's home when Leon first witnessed a baby being breast fed. On leaving the house, he immediately turned to me and, in a shocked tone, asked, 'did you see what that lady was doing?' I replied, 'yes, all babies are fed that way'. 'I wasn't', he retorted. 'Yes you were' I insisted. 'I was not'. 'Alright, we'll go home and ask mum'. So we raced home and as usual, mum was in the kitchen. 'Mum' I asked, 'when Leon was a baby, did you feed him up here?' and I indicated the breasts. The only term I knew for these parts was 'tits' and, in this situation, I was too embarrassed to say the word so resorted to the gesture. 'Yes' said mum, 'all babies eat that way'. Leon was sickened. He placed his hands on his stomach, bent over, and put on a gagging act. He was almost ill at this horrific enlightenment . . .

•

Waiting for the baby

Extracts from the account of Ursula during
her mother's pregnancy

(3;9)   U. was with her mother while she was bathing. Her mother said, U., *do you know what's in here?* 'No, what?' *Your little brother or sister.* She went very red and said in a weepy voice, '*Why*, Mummy? I don't want one while I'm little. I don't want one till I'm big.' This was repeated several times. Then followed various questions and comments: 'Why do you have it there?' *To keep it warm till it's ready to come out.* When will it come out? To-morrow? *No, not for a long time, not till the summer.* Why not? *It's not strong enough or big enough yet.* How big is it? *So big, I should think.* Where will it come out? *There.* How will it get out? *When it's big* enough and strong enough it'll push and I'll help it until it gets out. How will you push? *Like this.* How did you make it? Did Daddy plant a seed? *Yes.* When did he? Last night? *No, not then.* When we were on our holiday? *Perhaps.* Was I there? *No, I don't think so.* Was I asleep? *Perhaps?* Why did you make it? *Because I thought you would like a brother or sister to play with.* I like sisters best. How will you feed it? There? *Yes.* You could make a brother and a sister. *Could I?* One could feed that side and one could feed that side. Only they mustn't do a-a. *On me, do you mean?* In your lap. *I expect they will sometimes. They won't know when they're tiny.* We'll have to teach them.

'Mummy, what does my brother or sister do when you do a-a?' *Oh, it's all right. It's quite comfy. It just stays there.* How big is it now? So big – or so big? Let me feel. *I think it's a little bigger, about so big I should think.*

(3;10) 'Mummy, how did Daddy plant a seed in you?' *It's hard to explain, U. I must think of some way to explain so that you will understand it.* Tell me now, Mummy, how did he? *I promise to tell you later on. I can't until I think of a way to tell you.* I'll ask Daddy. He'll know. *Yes, perhaps he'll be able to explain.* He ought to know. He did it.

(3;10) Before going to sleep. U.: 'I want Daddy.' Her mother repeated what she thought she heard her say: *You want one Daddy.* One Daddy and one girl. *One Daddy and one girl.* Soon there will be one Daddy and two children. And then there will be one Daddy and three and . . . *I don't know whether I shall make three.* Daddy could. *Yes, Daddy could, but I should have to help him.* Why? *Well, I'd have to keep the baby in my tummy.* How does Daddy plant the seed, Mummy? *Oh, U., I must think of a way to explain it. It's a hard thing to explain.* Yes, but how, Mummy, how? Where does he keep the seed? *In his underneaths.* Why? *Oh, it's a good place to keep it.* How does he plant it? *He just puts it in.*

Where? *In my underneaths.* How does he? *He just pushes it in. And then I keep it in my tummy, and when it's ready it comes out and it's a baby and then it grows into a boy or girl and then into a man or woman.* And then *they* have babies! And that's how it goes on! (in a jolly voice as though reciting the end of 'The house that Jack built').

(3;11) At breakfast-time, U. was eating and watching her mother to see whose mouth was empty first. Hers was. She said, 'Mine's gone.' Her mother pinched her tummy and said, 'There!' She said, 'What's in my tummy, only food?' 'What's in yours? Mixed? Baby and food?' 'I wish . . . How is the seed planted? You did tell me. But how is it made?' *It grows inside Daddy.* Why does it? *Well it has to start somewhere.* Well, it could grow in the garden. *In the garden seeds of plants grow, not seeds of babies.* Well, it could, with others, and then you could pick out the seed of baby and plant it.

(4;8) Examining her person after a bath, U.: 'My underneath's got a tongue. Why has it?' M.: *It isn't really a tongue. It's a piece of flesh that looks like it.*

(5;1) U. (to M.): 'I love you very much. I love you so much that I sometimes cry because I don't want anybody else, only you. That shows how much I love you, doesn't it?' M.: *Does it?* Yes. *Well, I love you very much.* Well, I can't show how much you love me but I can show how much I love you.

(5;1) Something U. wanted her mother to do that she didn't want to do. U.: 'You *must*, Mummy, you *must*!' *Must I?* Yes, that's what Mummies are for, to do what their children want them to. *Is it?* Yes. And to look after them. *And what are children for?* To play, of course.

(5;3) U. (to Eileen, at teatime, provocatively): 'Can you see my botty?' (showing her bottom quickly and quickly pulling up her knickers). Eileen giggled. U. (continuing the game): 'You can't see my underneaths!' (Showing 'them' more obviously): 'Now you can. Touch them.' (E. tentatively touches.) U.: 'Not there, right inside.' E., 'I don't want to.'

Another time. U.: 'Shall we play botties?' (This game consists of pulling down one's knickers very quickly and pulling them up again, quickly saying, 'You can't see my botty,' and attempting to get a glimpse of the other person's in the brief opportunity allowed. She sometimes pulls up her mother's skirt and says, 'I can see your botty!' as though catching her mother out, looking gleeful and as though conscious of doing something forbidden. One of these occasions developed into an amusing and amused talk in the course of which her mother said U. had a very nice bottom. She said she didn't like it, and when her mother asked why, replied, 'Because it doesn't like to do "big".')

U. (to Nurse, and later told by U. to her mother, in the bathroom): 'Look, Nurse, I'm doing such a lovely thing. I'm putting the soap on my underneaths. It's lovely, so cool, shall I do it to R.?' Nurse: *No, she might not like it as you do.* When U. told her mother what a 'lovely thing' she'd done, her mother said, *On your underneaths?* U. said, 'No, inside. It was so nice.' *Why?* So cool.

(5;6) U.: 'The older I get the frightender I get. And the younger I am, the less frightened I am!'

•

Splints

From a mother's letter, 1933

I should like to ask your advice with regard to my little girl (age 3;9) who has contracted the habit of masturbation. This condition began about two years ago – and for the last 9 months I resorted to splints for her legs at night. This treatment resulted in the habit occurring during the day – if she was left alone to play – while previously it had only been noticed at bed time and during her afternoon rest. A few weeks ago I took her to a psychologist and nerve specialist – who advised me to discontinue the splints and her afternoon rest. I stay with her at night until she's asleep.

•

Not her fault

'Information from a woman acquaintance' of Susan Isaacs, child psychologist, 1933, England

1. At 5 years of age, playing in a field with a neighbour's son of 8 or 9 years, the boy exposed his genital fully and tried to persuade the girl to allow him to 'put it in'. She was shy and frightened and ran indoors.

2. At 8 years of age, after a picnic, she was left in a field with a boy of two years of age. She exposed the boy (still in petticoats) and tried to effect coitus. Her guilt about this incident was very great and remained even in adult life. She knew the boy and his parents at a later period of her own childhood, and could never see him or hear his name without feeling a pang of guilt and dread, lest she had done him some permanent harm. She always had the feeling that any illness the boy suffered from, or any difficulty with his parents, was her fault, and it was an immense relief to her when he grew up and she heard that he was doing well in business and in life generally.

•

A good game

From a letter to Susan Isaacs, child psychologist,
1933, England

I am so very much upset and worried over my little boy of 5
years old, Z. He is a very bright, handsome and affectionate
child – and everyone thinks him charming. He is an only boy,
with two little sisters, one older and one younger than him.
About a month ago I heard him say to his sister, 'I know a
good game' – then I heard laughter – then, 'I'll do it again.' I
looked in and to my horror saw him pull out his little penis and
jump up beside his sister who was reading on the sofa. I sent
him upstairs to bed, but next day when he was sent to the
lavatory, I heard him call, 'Come with me, B., and see my
"suckie" when I go to wee-wee.' I took him to his Daddy, who
spanked him and threatened to send him away to a school for
naughty rude boys. He wept bitterly and was most subdued for
a day and I did so hope it was but a transitory thing, and to-day
when I was getting their dinner ready and they were playing in
the next room with the door ajar I heard him say, 'Here, aren't I
pretty, would you like to look at this?' and saw him lift his
pinafore and start to undo his knickers!

•

Closely observed

Incidents in the lives of children aged between
two years eight months and four years eleven months,
from professional backgrounds

17.10.24.   The children plucked the withered hollyhock

stalks and used them to march round the garden in 'Follow my Leader'. There was a good deal of squabbling amongst the children as to whose were the longest of the sticks, everyone wanting these. Cecil was standing in the sand-pit with his own stick in his hand, and saw another child with one exactly similar in shape and size. Immediately, quite unaware of the stick he was holding, he shouted out, 'That's *mine*,' and tried to take it – looking surprised when we pointed out that he already had his.

22.1.25. Frank drew a crocodile. Dan at once made a plasticine crocodile 'to bite Mrs I.'.

3.2.25. The children drew crocodiles on the floor and the blackboard. Then, starting with Frank, the children were 'crocodiles' in turn, each chasing the others and pretending to bite.

9.2.25. Christoper drew a crocodile with a large mouth. Later Theobald drew a crocodile with a large mouth, which he said 'would bite Dan's legs off'.

25.2.25. Harold had accidentally kicked Mrs I.'s foot under the table, and this led him to say, 'I'll undress you and take off your suspenders, and gobble you all up.'

10.6.25. At lunch, Frank (5;8) said to Dan (4;1), 'Dan, yesterday I drank so much gas water (soda water) that I nearly blew up to the sky.' Dan replied without any pause, 'Frank, yesterday I ate so many potatoes that I nearly fell down to the ground.'

29.11.26. Conrad was playing happily with Jane and Dan, and said to Jane, 'When Lena makes anything and says, "Isn't this nice?" I say, "No, it's horrid," because I don't like Lena. I hate Lena, don't you?' Jane: 'Yes.'

In the evening, Conrad kicked the door, and said, 'That's to keep the ghosts out. There aren't any ghosts, are there, Jane?'

Jane replied, 'No, of course not. Have you ever seen a ghost, Miss D.?' 'No, Jane, I haven't.' Conrad then said, 'I expect *Lena* would have said, "Yes, I have."' Later, when they were using Meccano and talking, Dan said, 'I know someone I don't like,' and told the story of a girl who had pushed him in the street. Jane said, 'I know who I don't like. It's a girl.' Presently, Conrad: 'I know who you don't like, Jane, it's Priscilla.' Jane replied, 'Shan't tell you.' 'You used not to like her.' 'Well, I might have changed my mind.'

6.6.26.   When the children were playing at a journey game, Priscilla became 'a motor-bike' for a time, and lay on her face on the floor, with Dan 'riding' her, making thrusting movements with his loins, and showing sexual excitement – until Mrs I. intervened and suggested some other form of 'motor-bike'.

June, 1927.   At lunch, the children talked about 'the beginning of the world'. Dan (6;1) insists, whatever may be suggested as 'the beginning', that there must always have been 'something before that'. He said, 'You see, you might say that first of all there was a stone, and everything came from that – but (with great emphasis), *where did the stone come from*?' There were two or three variants on this theme. Then Jane (11;0), from her superior store of knowledge, said, 'Well, I have read that the earth was a piece of the sun, and that the moon was a piece of the earth'. Dan, with an air of eagerly pouncing on a fallacy, 'Ah! but where did *the sun* come from?' Tommy (5;4), who had listened to all this very quietly, now said with a quiet smile. '*I* know where the sun came from!' The others said eagerly, '*Do* you, Tommy? Where? Tell us'. He smiled still more broadly, and said, 'Shan't tell you!' to the vast delight of the others, who thoroughly appreciated this joke.

•

The twins

Experiences of Moshe Offer, aged twelve in 1944

We were taken out of the ghetto and placed in cattle cars. The journey took eight days – eight days without water, without food. It is painful for me to remember what went on there. It is too horrible to describe.

We arrived at Auschwitz in May 1944. I can even tell you the exact time: ten o'clock in the morning.

When they opened the doors to our cattle cars, there were a lot of dead children. During the trip, some mothers couldn't bear to hear the cries of their hungry babies – and so they killed them. I remember two blond, very beautiful children in my car whose mother had choked them to death because she could not stand to watch them suffer.

When we stepped off the trains, we could hear soldiers yelling, 'Men on one side, women on the other side.' Some German SS guards were also shouting, 'We want twins – bring us the twins!'

Dr Mengele was making the selections. He stood there, tall, nice-looking, and he was dressed very well, as if he wanted to make a good impression.

He had very soft hands, and he made fast decisions.

I heard my father cry out to them he had twins. He went over personally to Dr Mengele, and told him, 'I have a pair of twin boys.' Mengele sent some SS guards over to us. My twin, Tibi, and I were ordered to leave our parents and brothers and follow them.

But we didn't want to be separated from our mother, and so the Nazis separated us by force. My father begged Mengele to give us some food and water. But Mengele motioned to an SS guard, who beat him up on the spot.

As we were led away, I saw my father fall to the ground.

One morning, at roll call, my number and that of Tibi were announced as part of the group that was going for experiments. We were taken with some other children by ambulance to a laboratory. The doctors took many X rays of us.

Then, Dr Mengele walked in. He was wearing a white gown, but underneath his gown I could see his SS uniform and boots.

He gave me some candy, and then he gave me an injection that was extremely painful.

'*Nicht angst*,' Mengele told me in German. 'Don't be afraid.'

One day, my twin brother, Tibi, was taken away for some special experiments. Dr Mengele had always been more interested in Tibi. I am not sure why – perhaps because he was the older twin.

Mengele made several operations on Tibi.

One surgery on his spine left my brother paralyzed. He could not walk anymore.

Then they took out his sexual organs.

After the fourth operation, I did not see Tibi anymore.

I cannot tell you how I felt. It is impossible to put into words how I felt.

They had taken away my father, my mother, my two older brothers – and now, my twin.

I was in Mauthausen for about two or three weeks after the Death March. Then I was put along with other camp survivors on a train bound for I don't know where.

It was very crowded. I felt a push, and I fell off the train. To this day, I don't know if it was because I was so skinny, or because someone was trying to save me. In any case, I landed in a field. My hand was broken from the fall from the train.

I crawled through the field, and I looked up to see a big

German in uniform. I started crying and asked him to kill me. I told the Nazi I was a Jew. 'I fell off the train, and I cannot take it anymore, so go ahead and kill me.'

But the old German soldier said to me, 'I won't kill you – I am going to hide you.' And so he took me to an attic where they were storing corn and other grain.

This old German soldier was very nice. Every day, he brought me some dry biscuits and water. From the window of the attic, I saw the war coming to an end. I saw trains go by, carrying munitions. I watched German airplanes being shot down and parachutists jumping out – and being shot themselves.

One day, in the middle of the night, I heard artillery fire. After that night, the German didn't come anymore. I no longer got food or water. And so I began eating the corn and grain.

For four days, I was without any food or water. I was very hungry, very thirsty. But I stayed in the attic because I was also very frightened.

Then one day I looked out from the window and saw a jeep. It was carrying American soldiers. I was so weak, I couldn't walk, and so I crawled on my hands and knees from the attic to the jeep.

The American GIs spotted me and rescued me. They carried me in their arms to their jeep, and they gave me candy and chocolates.

•

The root of all evil

Story from a friend of Walter de la Mare, England, 1949

I was about four and a half, and can vividly remember a most discreditable incident. We were staying with a great aunt and one day she said to me that the love of money was the root of all evil. I knew the saying, but deliberately misunderstanding her, burst into floods of tears. I ran into the dining-room and hid under the table and howled. When made by my mother to explain the matter, I told them that 'old auntie' had said that Mummy was the root of all evil.

•

Circumcision

An account from the 1950s, Bethany, Palestine

For days before the operation the boy would be briefed by an uncle or a father about how to behave 'like a man'. A brave boy wasn't supposed to cry, even though the operation was performed with a simple razor and without anaesthetic: he was supposed to make a statement of courage as the razor was applied. Cousin Khalil Ibrahim managed to squeak, 'we are Hamads and we are accustomed to pain'. Cousin Khalil Mahmoud bettered him by declaring, 'this is for the eyes of my father'. Boys are praised or ridiculed in accordance with their behaviour in the shadow of the razor and one is either a goat or a lion forever as a result.

The mother's role up until the 1950s was an intriguing one, for she was the true organizer of this affair. Yet, she spent most of her time weeping, loudly and rightly bemoaning the pain which would be inflicted on her boy. Mothers, my grandmother Rashedah included, are known to have gone to visit the neighbours at that moment of utmost delicacy, 'because she didn't want to see her children in pain'. Aunt Nafisa Ali went into her usual hysterics when her only son was the centre of the affair; uncle Ibrahim, a man who never suffered women's sobbing gladly, told her very seriously to stop it because, 'her son's wasn't the only cock in the family. How else is he going to become a man?'

•

A joke

Recorded by an American psychologist

At a quarter past three there was only one child left in the kindergarten classroom, the others having been called for by mothers or maids or older brothers or sisters. The teacher came over to where the little boy sat quietly waiting and asked with some solicitude: 'Who is calling for you today, Eugene? Your mother? Or Betty?' The boy smiled: 'My mother is coming, and Betty is coming, and Kay is coming – the whole family is coming except me because I'm here already.' He laughed.

In this joke the little boy transformed an anxious feeling into one of amusement. Let us see how this has come about. He takes the teacher's question as an occasion for reversing the situation, as if to say: It is only you and not I who is worried whether anyone is coming to call for me – and how ridiculous you are to doubt it. He is helped to this retort by a rather precocious tendency to turn what the teacher says into nonsense. Here he says something nonsensical himself (I am not coming because I am already here) in order to make nonsense of the teacher's concern.

But to understand Eugene's little joke more fully we must know that his father has died in the past year. The thought 'the whole family is coming' contains the wish: and my father too. This is immediately renounced with the word 'except': the whole family is coming except one. But what would have been a direct expression of the sad reality is in its turn warded off with the substitution of himself for his father. Instead of 'all except Daddy because he is dead,' he produces 'all except me because I'm here already.' This gives the impression of being nonsense as he pretends to convey information while what he says is self-evident. The little boy's substitution of himself for his father in the joke repeats what has happened in life: the father has died and the five-year-old boy has been left alone with the mother and two older sisters. The nonsense in the joke expresses the thought: But it is nonsense to suppose that I could take my father's place. As in the case of nonsense in dreams, it represents opposed wishes: I did and did not wish for my father's death. Thus the nonsense has a double application: the boy disposes of the doubt – which he imputes to the teacher – that anyone is coming for him; and, on a deeper level, he repudiates the wish to take his father's place. In yet another way this joke may have served to ward off anxiety. Waiting for his mother or sister the little boy may indeed have wondered whether they were ever coming, whether they might not also be dead. And this may have evoked fears of his own death. In saying, 'I am here,' he is affirming: I am alive.

•

An experiment

The 1950s in a state school for mentally handicapped
children in Massachusetts, reported in
the *Boston Globe* and then the *Guardian*, 6 January 1994

Nearly 200 children – some of them as young as three years old – were given high doses of the blood pressure medication Reserpine to see if it curbed disturbing behavioural problems.

'A published study of the drug test makes no mention of obtaining consent,' the newspaper report said. 'It states only that 188 residents "were selected for this study because they presented social or emotional problems".'

•

Revolutionary priorities

An experience of Jung Chang in China, 1950s

My family life was tranquil and loving. Whatever resentment my mother felt for my father, she seldom had rows with him, at least not in front of the children. My father's love for us was rarely shown through physical contact now that we were older. It was not customary for a father to hold his children in his arms, or to show affection by kissing them or embracing them. He would often give the boys piggyback rides, and would pat their shoulders or stroke their hair, which he rarely did to us girls. When we got beyond the age of three he would lift us carefully with his hands under our armpits, strictly adhering to Chinese convention, which prescribed avoiding intimacy with one's daughters. He would not come into the room where my sister and I slept without our permission.

My mother did not have as much physical contact with us as she would have liked. This was because she fell under another set of rules: those of the Communists' puritanical life-style. In the early 1950s, a Communist was supposed to give herself so completely to the revolution and the people that any demonstration of affection for her children was frowned on as a sign of divided loyalties. Every single hour apart from eating or sleeping belonged to the revolution, and was supposed to be spent working. Anything that was regarded as not to do with the revolution, like carrying your children in your arms, had to be dispatched with as speedily as possible.

At first, my mother found this hard to get used to. 'Putting family first' was a criticism constantly leveled at her by her Party colleagues. Eventually, she became drilled into the habit of working nonstop. By the time she came home in the evening, we had long since gone to sleep. She would sit by our bedsides watching our faces as we slept and listening to our peaceful breathing. It was the happiest moment in her day.

Whenever she had time she would cuddle us, gently scratching or tickling us, especially on our elbows, which was intensely pleasurable. Pure heaven for me was putting my head on her lap and having the inside of my ears tickled. Ear-picking was a traditional form of pleasure for the Chinese. As a child, I remember seeing professionals carrying a stand with a bamboo chair on one end and scores of tiny fluffy picks dangling from the other.

•

My friend Billy

A playground rhyme by a ten-year-old girl,
Northern Ireland, 1958

> My friend Billy's got a ten foot willy,
> he showed it to the girl next door.
> She thought it was a snake
> so she hit it with a rake,
> and now it's only four foot four.

•

Toast

A poem by Maureen Natt, England, 1970s

> I remember my Dad he was the best Dad
> anyone could have
> When my sister and I were young
> We had such fun.
> When my Mum went out for a drink,

which she did most nights,
My Dad would get out the bread
and toast it on the fire for us.
We thought this was a great treat,
with cheese on top
We would sit and he would tell us stories
of when he was a lad.
I have tasted toast which other people have made
But it wasn't as good as my Dad's.

•

November 1975

A conversation between Natasha, aged six, and Adam,
aged eight, recorded by R. D. Laing

November 1975
Same evening. Later

Natasha	I wish I could marry you daddy
Daddy	Oh Natasha. We can't
Natasha	I know because you're married to mummy
Daddy	even if I weren't we couldn't because you're my daughter and I'm your daddy and daughters and daddys aren't allowed to get married
Natasha	we're in the same family
Daddy	yes
Natasha	but mummy's in the same family, so how can you be married to her?
Daddy	when mummy and I met she wasn't your mummy and we were not members of the same family and she isn't my daughter so it was alright to get married and have children
Adam	by putting your penis into mummy's vagina

Daddy   and become a family and get married
Jutta   it's bedtime now
Daddy   yes it's past your bedtime
Natasha   but I'm not sleepy
Daddy   I never said you were. Anyway. Kisses. (*kisses*) and
           you're to go through to your room and be quiet
Adam   (*kissing Jutta*) Natasha would like to marry daddy, and
           I would like to marry you.

•

Hunch Bunch

A playground rhyme by a girl aged twelve,
London, 1977

Hunch Bunch, call the Judge,
Mother's having a baby.
Is it a boy?
Is it a girl?
Is it a human baby?

Wrap it up in tissue paper.
Throw it down the escalator.
First floor – drop.
Second floor – drop.
Third floor – kick the door.
Mother's not having a baby no more.

•

Coming home

A poem by Brenda Dundas, aged thirteen, London, 1977

Coming Home on my own Thinking
Couldn't Wait to get home Thinking
Buzzing of the planes engines Thinking
Couldn't wait to meet me friends Thinking
I'll miss this cold country Thinking
Coming home Guyana Thinking
Back to the nice warm weather Thinking.

•

What parents say

Parents' irritating sayings, collected by children
aged twelve and thirteen at Toot Hill Comprehensive School,
Bingham, Nottinghamshire, England, 1978

Isn't it time you thought about bed?
  It must be somewhere
You speak to him Harold, he won't listen to me.
  Who do you think I am?
You'd better ask your father
  It's late enough as it is
Don't eat with your mouth open
  In this day and age
Did anybody ask your opinion
  I remember when I was a boy
  And after all we do for you
You're not talking to your school friends now you know
  Why don't you do it the proper way
  I'm only trying to tell you
  What did I just say
  Now, wrap up warm

B.E.D. spells bed
Sit up straight and don't gobble your food
For the five hundredth time
Don't let me ever see you do that again.
Have you made your bed?
Can't you look further than your nose?
No more lip
Have you done your homework?
Because I say so.
Don't come those fancy ways here
Any more and you'll be in bed
My, haven't you grown
Some day I won't be here, then you'll see
A chair's for sitting on
You shouldn't need telling at your age.
Want, want, want, that's all you ever say

•

In the playground

Children describe their new song-and-dance
to Iona Opie, England, 1978

A scurry of girls arrived. 'Will you write, "Paul Colston is a
fool," and "Richard Williams is a twit"? Go on, *please*. Put it in
the paper. They've been laughing at our song we've been
making up. We learnt it from Tracey. She had it from her big
sister. We knew a lot of it already, but we learnt the other little
bits. We learnt it last week, and we kept doing it and then we
learnt other people. We'll show you.' They stood in two lines
facing each other and went into a song-and-dance routine:

In and out of the red balloon [move toward partner, clap
hands together, retreat, describe balloon in air with hands]

Marry the farmer's daughter [link arms with partner, go round
    and back to place]

Sleepyhead in the afternoon [hands together as pillow, rock
    head]

Britannia, Britannia [fling right arm round and back, then
    left]

Melissa [both arms round and back]

Sleepyhead in the afternoon [as before, then turn facing
    outwards]

My – name – is

Diana Dors, I'm a movie star [jump round to face partner
    again]

I wear long johns and I play the guitar [suitable motions
    while swaying to rhythm]

I've got the legs, the legs [legs forward in turn]

The hips, the hips [smooth the hips each side]

Turn around movie star, hey hey! [twirl round, throw hands
    in air at 'hey hey!']

See those girls in red, white, and blue [move forward, winding
    fists round each other]

See the boys say 'How do you do?' [return to line, unwinding
    fists]

So – keep the sunny side, keep the sunny side, keep the sunny
    side up, up,

And the other side too, too [jump, crossing and uncrossing
    the feet, kick legs in air at 'up, up' and 'too, too', clapping
    under legs]

See the soldiers marching along,

Elvis Presley singing a song,

So – keep the sunny side, keep the sunny side, keep the sunny
    side up, up,

And the other side too, too. [actions as before]

'The words mean nothing, really. We just made them up.' But
this applies only to the first six lines. 'My name is Diana Dors'
has been a popular dance routine since at least 1966, and 'Keep

the sunny side up' since at least 1960. It took some time to set down the words and actions. They could not think of either without performing the dance from the beginning, and I could not write and describe the actions for more than two lines at once.

•

In the news

Iona Opie records children in a playground

Paul's brother was waiting to meet me round by the senior classrooms (the bell had gone). 'I was wanting to tell you this story,' he said seriously. 'There was this man, OK? and he was in love with this lady, and 'e 'ad it off with this lady, and the lady's husband come home —' Some of the other boys were beginning to laugh. Paul's brother rounded on them. 'This is really true, OK?' he said fiercely. 'Yes, it was in the papers,' one of the boys said, supporting him. 'Well,' said Paul's brother, ''E 'ad it off with 'er, and the husband come home —' 'I heard that one, it was ages ago,' said another boy. Paul's brother did not take any notice. 'And the husband cut the man's willy off, and the police come and they had to go looking for it.' 'Yes, that's right,' said a boy. 'It was in the *Sun*.'

I found myself facing a primitive figure in a worn duffle coat. 'I wondered what you are playing,' I said in the dream-like voice I often use, as if I was part of their game already. 'We're playing Anti-tanks and Anti-aeroplanes,' he said. 'We're killing elephants and the warring mammoths. We're trying to kill them, anyway. That's how they got extinct.'

•

Moving in

A poem by Marisa Horsford, aged ten,
Nottingham, 1970s

Moving out
Of an old crowd
trying
to move
Into a new crowd
But no one
wants to know
you
At all.

But when
you make them
feel stupid
And make them
look small
Everybody
wants to be your friend
Everybody
wants to be your friend
Everyone around
you
You seem to know.

Every morning

A poem by Keith Ballentine, aged twelve, London, 1979

Every morning on a Saturday and Sunday
I go to my paper round at 6.30 a.m.
and by 7.00 I am back home
and I go back to bed to get some sleep.
I make a little bit of noise
when I get into bed,
and just when I am dozing off,
my brother wakes up.
He knows I am awake
and he wants me to stay awake
so he goes outside for a pee –
I know that, because I can hear him
flush the toilet.
Then he bursts inside
and stands in front of the mirror
and says, 'SPIDER MAN!!!'

●

Moon man

Five-year-olds talking, America 1981

Earl: My cousin says you can wish on the man in the
             moon. I told my mother and she says it's only
             pretend.
Wally: He doesn't have a face or a body.
Lisa: Then he can't see. He's not real.
Deana: But how could he get in?
Wally: With a drill.

Eddie: The moon won't break. It's white like a ghost. The drill would pass in but no hole will come out.

Earl: There can't be a moon man because there's no door. How would he get in?

Wally: Maybe there's a secret passageway.

Teacher: Who made it?

Wally: The moon man.

Kenny: There *is* a face but my daddy says when you get up there it's just holes. Why would that be?

Deana: Somebody could be up there making a face and then when somebody goes up there he's gone.

Lisa: He might have left a hole from last time.

Fred: There can't be a moon man. It's too round. He'd fall off.

Wally: He can change his shape. He gets rounder.

Eddie: The astronauts didn't change their shape. They had oxygen for the air. In machines.

Fred: I saw that on television. They were walking on the moon. But a real moon man would have to find a door. And if you fall in a hole you'll never get out.

Andy: Sure you can, when the moon is a tiny piece.

Warren: There *is* such a thing as a half moon. But the astronauts can't be cut in half. They can only go when it's round. A moon man can squeeze in half.

Wally: That's what I said. He's a round shape or half a round. But I never saw a door.

Eddie: There's no air there. No air! But air is invisible so how can there be no air?

Wally: Only the moon man sees it. He makes himself invisible so he can see it.

Earl: My cousin says you can wish on him.

Wally: The moon is right next to God so he could talk to God.

Tanya: Maybe there's a moon fairy, because some fairies are white that you could see through.

Lisa: He could be a different kind of fairy – the kind for up
            there.

The going rate for an 'easy to place baby' – a euphemism
for a white, blond-haired, blue-eyed male child less than
five months old – is $25,000. Older children, female or
dark-skinned babies cost proportionately less.

Caroline Blackwell, ed., *Betrayal*

Greed

A poem by John Hegley

Once when I wanted all my sister's sweets
I pretended to be a hungry dog
and each time she dropped one on the floor
I amused her with my comical scavenging
and when all her sweets had gone
I stopped and got on with my own
taking no interest in the hungry dog
that looked very much like my sister.

•

One of the wise men

Black children in a Nativity play:
Gary Younge, *Guardian*, 1993

And I thought I had been blessed. While all the other children
battled it out to play shepherds and angels in my infant school's

nativity play, the teacher had decided, without a moment's hesitation, that I was destined to be a wise man.

With the innocence of a five-year-old I concluded that I must be a natural. Only 19 years later, while helping out at a playgroup for black children in Edinburgh, would I learn the truth. All the boys in the group – and even some of the girls – were wise men that year. When I told my two brothers they confessed that they too had been told to come from the East . . .

In short, some people believe there are certain things black people can and should do and others that they cannot. So deeply can this be entrenched that they cannot even imagine them doing anything else. Which explains why there are so many young black royals this year. The Kings came from afar. Legend has it that at least one of them was black; and the chances of any of them being Caucasian are pretty slim.

•

Mam

A poem to her mother by Mary Bell, aged thirteen,
two years after being convicted of the manslaughter
of two boys, aged four and three, 1970

Mam
I know that in my heart
From you once was not apart
My love for you grows
More each day
When you visit me mam
I'd weep once your away
I look into your eyes, so blue and they're very sad. You try to be
    very cheery But I know you think Im Bad so Bad
though I really dont know If You feel the same,
 and treat it as a silly game.

a child who has made criminal fame
Please mam put my tiny mind at ease
tell judge and jury on your knees they will LISTEN to your cry of
    PLEAS
THE GUILTY ONE IS you not me.
I SORRY IT HAS TO BE THIS WAY
Well both cry and you will go away to other gates where you are free
    locked up in prison cells.
Your famley are wee.
these last words I speak, on behalf of dad, Patrick, [brother] and me
    tell them you are guilty
Please, so then mam, Ill be free,
Daughter May

•

Sunday school teacher

Poem by Robin, aged ten, England, 1972

Mrs Nunn
Please talk to me.
You always seem to pray
In Sunday school.
When I go to talk to you, you say time to pray
You give us our scriptures, when I go to say
What is the time
You say read the back of the scripture
Tig tig as you tap the side of a cup
Time to go home you
Say in a kind voice.
Now is my time to talk to you
God comes first she said.

•

A hero

Five-year-olds talking, America, 1981

Wally: My mom said Martin Luther King was smart and he decided about having white people to sit in the front and black people in the back. Wait! That was what *they* decided. And then *he* decided to throw off that sign and so you could sit anywhere.

Eddie: You forgot to say about Rosa Parks. See, she came on the bus and gave the bus driver some money and she sat in the chair and the bus driver said, 'No, you're not white.' And she said, 'I don't care. I want to sit because I'm tired and also I gave you a dime.' Was it a dime or a nickel?

Tanya: Maybe a quarter.

Eddie: Maybe a dime. So she said, 'I'm not going to leave.' So they put her in jail.

Wally: Now you can sit wherever you want. Also Martin wasn't allowed to go to any water fountain or any bathroom and he also had to have only a black grocery-store man to pay. He was separated. My mom knows all about that. She even used to *be* separated.

Eddie: We're talking about the bus now, Wally. He told people they shouldn't go on the bus and don't pay them money. Then if they get a broken bus they can't fix it.

Warren: And he told them to stop shopping if you can only be white.

Wally: I want to tell the part about when he was in kindergarten. Tommy's mother said, 'Go away, bad boy.' And he said, 'I'm his friend.' And she said, 'No, you're the wrong color.' He was only a little boy so he cried. So he went to his mother and she said, 'I have to tell you something sad. There's a rule against us.'

Rose: Why did they have that?

Wally: It was their habit. Anyway Martin changed all the rules.

Lisa: All the *bad* rules.

Fred: But not the one for the bathroom. The girls have to separate from the boys.

•

Santa Claus

Five-year-olds talking, America, 1981

Rose: I saw a black Santa Claus and a white Santa Claus.

Kenny: He can't be black. He has to be only white.

Rose: I saw him at Sears.

Warren: Santa Claus is white.

Wally: If you're black, Santa Claus is black, and if you're white, Santa Claus is white. But I think he's white.

Teacher: But aren't you black, Wally?

Wally: I know. But I see Santa Claus and he's white.

Deana: There's both kinds. Because we went to Sears and saw a white Santa so the black one must have been sick.

Earl: He's very white. My sister said he's a spirit and spirits are white.

Teacher: Why can't a spirit be black?

Earl: I'm not black so I don't know.

Tanya: I haven't seen a black Santa Claus but I know he could be there, because everything comes in black or white. (*She looks around.*) Or Japanese. Or Chinese.

Eddie: No. I know only one color he should be. White. I saw him in the store.

Teacher: But Rose *saw* a black Santa.

Eddie: He could have been dressing up like a black Santa.

Wally: Did he talk, Rose? Maybe he had wires.

Rose: He said, 'Ho, ho, ho!'

Wally: I think he was real.

Tanya: If he was real that means someone was dressed up like Santa Claus because he lives at the North Pole and he can't come here. Maybe he has other people meet the children while he stays there.

Teacher: Is the Santa at the North Pole white or black?

Tanya: There's two. The white Santa Claus goes to meet the children and the black one stays at the North Pole.

Wally: He's magic.

Andy: Wally's right! He changes colors. That's how it's done.

Eddie: Now I get it! He's a magician.

Tanya: See, someone must be dressed up to be a certain kind of Santa Claus. If they need a white one, *he* comes out. If they need a black one, *he* comes out.

•

The tooth gazelle

Iraqi boy's account of what to do when
a child loses a tooth, 1981

The child throws the tooth towards the sun and says in Arabic, 'Oh sun, take this donkey's tooth and give me a gazelle's tooth.'

•

Getting the point

A group of American five-year-olds, 1981

Shortly after we read 'The Three Pigs', this conversation took place.

Andy: There's a boy Jeffrey on the other block from me. I went to his house once and he wouldn't let me in.

Lisa: Why?

Andy: Someone else was there.

Wally: You should have gone down the chimney.

Lisa: You shouldn't sneak into someone's house.

Eddie: He should shape his hair in a different way and then come back and Jeffrey'll say 'Come in' and tell the other boy to go home.

Fred: If he went down the chimney he might get boiled.

Wally: He could come down with a gun.

Eddie: Just to scare him. If he puts a boiling pot there, just jump over it.

Lisa: Not a gun.

Eddie: Here's a great idea. Get bullets and put it in the gun and aim it at Jeffrey.

Teacher: That's a great idea?

Eddie: No, I mean it's a bad idea.

Lisa: Well, let him come down the chimney but not with a gun.

Wally: Let's all go to Jeffrey's house and climb down his chimney and make him let Andy come in.

Andy: I'll find out if he has a chimney.

Wally: I'll get a time-out chimney and he has to stay in there until he lets you come in.

Note:

time out: withdrawn for punishment by teacher, parent or referee

•

Bad guy

Four-year-olds in Chicago, America, 1980s

Emily has seen a television program that confuses and worries her. The terrain is unfamiliar, the fears so strange they cannot be disguised. Yet, in three consecutive days of acting out the unknown, the girls find a means of taking control: *they invent the bad guy*.

First Day

Emily:	Do you want to have boyfriends?
Mollie:	Are we sisters?
Emily:	My boyfriend Derek is coming to kiss me. Do you want to play that?
Margaret:	Can I do that too?
Emily:	What's your boyfriend's name?
Margaret:	I don't know. Tell me what.
Emily:	Do you want Derek or Steven?
Margaret:	Derek or Steven.
Emily:	Okay, Derek. He's coming to kiss you on your body.
Margaret:	Only on my cheek. Not on my body.
Emily:	Then you can't have it. That's not sexy. Only on your body is sexy.
Mollie:	To be kissed on your body?
Emily:	Okay, nobody will kiss me. I'm going to be on a date. I'm going to be on the camping. Tell Derek

it's time for me to go to bed when he comes here, all right?

Mollie: Does he come to the camping?

Emily: If he comes here when we sleep he might take me, right?

Mollie: This is my pillow. My baby is on the pillow with me.

Second Day

Emily: This time I'm not having boyfriends.

Mollie: Why?

Emily: Okay, I will.

Margaret: Am I still the Derek?

Emily: I'm taking my baby along. A lot of boyfriends are in this room. I'm moving to the other room. Come on, sisters. Let's take all the clothes into the other room. (*The girls move armfuls of clothing and purses to the cubby room.*)

Mollie: Does the boyfriend find us?

Emily: We're packing up and we're going because we don't want boyfriends anymore. There's no girlfriends here. Only there could be sisters.

Margaret: We don't like boyfriends anymore, right, Emily? So we're moving to sisters?

Mollie: We need a mother to pretend. We need a real mother. For the moving. You can't move without a mother to know where you are. Call me the mother only for now.

Emily: Goodbye, mother. We're not going to come here again. I don't like my boyfriend. Derek wants to do something I don't know what it is.

Margaret: I'm tired, mother. Cover me up. Put my baby here.

Third Day

Emily: We're going on a camping and we're going to stay there. I'll call your boyfriends and tell them.

Mollie: Who?

Emily: Derek. Do you still love him?

Mollie: Who?

Emily: Derek. Does he still love you?

Mollie: Who?

Emily: Derek. But don't let him see me because I'm a very little girl now. I used to be big.

Margaret: Who's the boyfriend that doesn't like you anymore? Mollie could be it.

Emily: Oh no, he wants to come! Derek wants to come! Oh, no, he's coming!

Mollie: (*Frightened*) You better hide.

Margaret: Call your boyfriend that doesn't love you anymore. Tell him we're on a camping trip!

Emily: Mollie! Your boyfriend is here! Excuse me. We can't have you for this place because the girls are sleeping here. Oh, no! The boyfriend stoled all our clothes. Oh, no, my purse is stoled!

Mollie: Oh no, my dress is gone!

Margaret: The fire is out. He took the fire out! He took the rug out so the fire will come out. Call the police. There he's coming in here!

Emily: Help me, help me! He's just a real bad guy! Mollie, did you see that? A bad guy! Hit him with the purse.

Mollie: Oh no! Bad guy, bad guy, bad guy, bad guy!

Their screams ricochet through the room. They begin throwing clothing and purses at the unseen villain, then fall into one another's arms, aglow with fright and relief.

•

Skipping song

A song by ten-year-old girls in Harlem, New York City,
in the 1980s, collected by Karol Swanson

> Kiss my acker-backer
> my soda cracker
> my B, U, T
> my doodie-hole
> your ma
> your pa
> your greasy granny
> wears dirty panties
> gotta big behind
> like Frankenstein
> gotta root-toot-toot
> like a prostitute
> gotta ding dong
> like King Kong
> gotta beat-beat
> on Sesame Street.

●

S-t-r-e-t-c-h-i-n-g

A poem by Sharon Cheeks, aged about ten,
London, 1982

> Waking up
> in the morning
> is lovely.
> Especially when you s-t-r-e-t-c-h.
> You open up

your legs and arms
and stretch.
It's just lovely.
The feeling just makes
you want to do it
over and over again.
But after a while
your stretch
runs out
and it's over.

•

My memories

A poem by Tanweer Khaled, aged about twelve,
London, 1984

Bangladesh
I remember going to my village home
I remember it being hot
I remember the soles of my shoes
burning up on the hot road
I remember jumping about because
of my hot foot
I remember my little brother
running up to my grandparents
on his little feet like an ant
I remember my little brother
jumping on my grandfather's lap
and my grandfather nearly falling
off the chair
I remember having a nice meal
I remember my brother eating
the leg of a chicken like a lion

eating a deer
I remember the homemade ovens
I remember . . . I remember . . .
I remember . . . I remember BANGLADESH

•

Understanding

Leanne Platek, in Staffordshire, aged eleven,
during the Miners' Strike, Great Britain, 1984–5

This strike means a lot to me and my dad because he and all
other men who are on strike are fighting against job losses and
for their children's future. Although I am eleven I understand
most of the strike. I like going on the picket line with my mum
and dad and friends, and the boys in blue watching us. Also
going on marches holding placards with COAL NOT DOLE and
SAVE JOBS.

•

Bed!

A poem by Joni Akinrele from Benthal Primary School,
Hackney, London, 1984

When it is time to go to bed
my mum says:
'BED!'
I say:
'Please can I stay up
until this film finishes?'
'What time does it finish?' my mum says.

'Ten o'clock,' I say.
'No way,' my mum says.
'Oh can't I stay up for five minutes?'
'No.'
'Please.'
'No!'
'Oh . . . can't I read in bed?'
'No!'
'Please.'
'Come here, girl . . . You are getting on my nerves
if you are not in that bed
by the time I count to . . .'

I walk slowly up the stairs
my brother is laughing away.
Then my mum starts shouting again.
This time at my brother.

●

Why?

A poem by Ben Bruton, Wood's Foundation
Church of England School, 1985

When the vase gets broken,
                why do I always get the blame?
When the garden's untidy,
                why do I have to clear it up?
When the book gets ripped,
                why do I have to mend it?
When someone breaks the pencil lead,
                why do I get the blame?
When the newspaper gets lost,
                why do I have to find it again?

I can answer all these questions.

Because I broke the vase
Because I made the garden untidy
Because I ripped the book
Because I broke the pencil lead
Because I lost the paper.

•

Freedom

A poem by Moagi, aged about seven, South Africa, 1980s

When I am old I would like to have
a wife and two children
a boy and a girl and a big house
and two dogs and freedom
my friends and I would like to meet together

•

Song

A playground rhyme by girls aged seven, London, 1985

My boyfriend gave me an apple,
my boyfriend gave me a pear,
my boyfriend gave me a kiss on the lips
and threw me down the stairs.

I gave him back his apple,
I gave him back his pear,
I gave him back his kiss on the lips
and I threw him down the stairs.

He took me to the pictures,
to see a sexy film,

and when I wasn't looking
he kissed another girl.

I threw him over Italy,
I threw him over France.
I threw him over Germany
and he landed on his arse.

•

Typically middle-class

Sarah Hobson reporting in
'Battered and abused children', Great Britain, 1980s

Age: nineteen. Sex: female. Occupation: shop manageress.

People ask: what kind of families? Well, my family was typically middle-class with a detached house in the country, two cars, and holidays every year. There were two brothers and a sister, all a lot older than me. I was the baby, the only one that spent time with my parents.

My father was a large man who was physically very powerful. When he hit me I was flung the length of the room. He was a respected man, a manager who owned his own business. My mother was a quiet, cold woman who worked part-time because she wanted to – not because she had to.

When I was small she undressed me and locked me in the coal bunker. When she took me out she told me off for being dirty and put me in a red-hot bath of water.

I was seven when my father first raped me. I was nine when he had anal intercourse with me. His visits to my room were part of my life. At fourteen I had a miscarriage. After that I tried to commit suicide several times. I was put in a psychiatric hospital for several months when I was seventeen.

A summary of the United Nations Convention on the Rights of the Child, 1989

- Children are defined as those under the age of 18, unless national laws fix an earlier age of majority.

- Every child has the inherent right to life, and States shall ensure to the maximum child survival and development.

- Every child has the right to a name and nationality from birth.

- When courts, welfare institutions or administrative authorities deal with children, the child's best interests shall be a primary consideration. The child's opinions shall be given careful consideration.

- States shall ensure that each child enjoys full rights without discrimination or distinctions of any kind.

- Children shall not be separated from their parents, unless by competent authorities for their well-being; States should facilitate reunification of families by permitting travel in or out of their borders.

- Parents have the primary responsibility for a child's upbringing, but States shall provide them with appropriate assistance and develop child-care institutions.

- States shall provide parentless children with suitable alternative care. The adoption process shall be carefully regulated and international agreements should be sought to provide safeguards and assure legal validity if and when adoptive parents intend to move the child from his or her country of birth.

- Disabled children shall have the right to special treatment, education and care.

- The child is entitled to the highest attainable standard of health. States shall ensure that health care is provided to all children, placing emphasis on preventive measures, health education and reduction of infant mortality.

- Primary education shall be free and compulsory as early as possible; discipline should respect the child's dignity. Education should prepare the child for life in a spirit of understanding, peace and tolerance.

- Children shall have time to rest and play and equal opportunities for cultural and artistic activities.

- States shall protect the child from economic exploitation and work that may interfere with education or be harmful to health and well-being.

- States shall protect children from the illegal use of drugs and involvement in drug production or trafficking.

- All efforts shall be made to eliminate the abduction and trafficking of children.

- Capital punishment or life imprisonment shall not be imposed for crimes committed before the age of 18. Children in detention should be separated from adults; they must not be tortured or suffer cruel or degrading treatment.

- No child shall take any part in hostilities; children exposed to armed conflict shall receive special protection.

- Children of minority and indigenous populations shall freely enjoy their own culture, religion and language.

- Children who have suffered maltreatment, neglect or detention should receive appropriate treatment or training for recovery and rehabilitation.

● States should make the Convention's rights widely known to
both adults and children and undertake the legislative and
administrative measures necessary for their implementation.

Included in Anuradha Vittachi, *Stolen Childhood*

I a boy one witch

Sarah Hobson reporting in
'Battered and abused children', Great Britain, 1980s

Age: three. Sex: male. Adopted.

Daddy got dangerous fingers. Daddy has. He's got some nails,
big nails. Put them up my back. Make it bleed.

My mummy got the fag and burns me and Colin's back.
Right up there, up my head. And down my leg, and burnt my
shoes. My best shoes.

My mummy, her put a fag up my bottom.

My daddy in my bedroom. Him clown. Him getting me.

My daddy pull my willy. My bleed on my bottom.

Daddy hurt me. Him not love me. I horrible, him say.

Daddy, Kevin, Gary, Maxine, Glenys, Sam, David, Debbie,
Grandad. Them witches.

Them get spiders and worms in black boxes. Put them in our
hair.

Them witches burning me. Me and Craig and Darren.

Them witches make you go in the bonfire. It burns us. When

them splash you with water, you stronger and stronger. Can't get burnt. Them witches splash you with water.

Mum know them witches.

I a boy one witch.

•

A dream

A poem by Ho Foong Ling, aged about ten,
Singapore, 1985

One night
after going to a fancy-dress party
dressed as a carrot
I saw a giant rabbit.
It thought I was his dinner.

While I was running away from it,
I fell.
I could not get up.
My leg bled
The giant rabbit hopped nearer to me.
It opened his mouth
and wanted to eat me up.
When his teeth touched my head
I woke up
and found myself on the floor.
I think that must have happened
when I fell.

•

Detention

Anne Chisholm in 'Children in prison',
on an Indian 'child care home', 1980s

One of the girls stayed behind to talk to us. She was about
eight, slender and pretty, with a long neck, pigtails tied with
red ribbons and a dazzling smile. Her nickname was Baby.
Mrs Mitra asked her how she had found herself in gaol, and
translated her answers for me. Baby did not seem reluctant to
answer but gazed trustingly at Mrs Mitra and spoke without
hesitation.

'She was on a bus with her mother,' said Mrs Mitra, 'and her
mother got off the bus to get some water. She got off and never
came back, and Baby was left in the bus. Someone took her
from the bus and she went to court next day, and then she was
sent to Presidency Gaol.' How long was she there? 'She's not
sure. Quite a long time.' What happened to her in the gaol?
Could she remember what she did all day? 'She was not really
studying, but singing, playing games, playing with toys.' What
did she feel when she moved from the gaol to the Child Care
Home? 'She says it's quite different here and she likes it better.
She especially likes dancing and going to school.' What would
she like to do when she grows up? 'She wants to do housework',
said Mrs Mitra laughing. 'And also be a dancing teacher.'

•

On the streets

An account by Andrea di Robilant of
street children in Brazil, 1980s

. . . twelve-year-old Teresa wandered barefoot into the hospital
carrying a stinking bundle in her arms. She asked the doctors
what was wrong with her child. They unwrapped the bundle
and found a tiny, decomposing corpse. The baby was a month
old: she had died of infections around her anus and her vagina.
The acid of urine and faeces had corroded the flesh to such an
extent that the bones stuck out. José Nelson de Freitas covered
his face as he told me the story. 'She had never changed those
filthy wrappings. Never once cleaned the child. She thought the
baby was a doll! When we told her it was dead she sobbed and
had nervous convulsions. We calmed her down with sedatives.
Four hours later she slipped out of the hospital and went back
to the square.'

•

Song

A playground song from a London girl aged seven, 1985

> When Suzy was a baby,
> a baby Suzy was,
> she went ga ga
> a ga-ga-ga
> a ga ga ga ga ga-ga-ga.
>
> When Suzy was a toddler,
> a toddler Suzy was,
> she went scribble, scribble

scribble-scribble-scribble
scribble scribble scribble-scribble-scribble.

When Suzy was a Junior,
a Junior Suzy was,
she went Miss, Miss,
I need to go a piss,
I don't know where the toilet is.

When Suzy was a Secondary,
a Secondary Suzy was,
she went ooh ah,
I've lost my bra,
I left my knickers in my boyfriend's car.

When Suzy was a mummy,
a mummy Suzy was,
she went sh sh sh-sh-sh
sh sh sh sh sh-sh-sh. (rocking baby)

When Suzy was a granny,
a granny Suzy was,
she went knit knit knit-knit-knit
knit knit knit knit knit-knit-knit.

When Suzy was a skeleton,
a skeleton Suzy was,
she went rattle rattle rattle-rattle-rattle
rattle rattle rattle-rattle-rattle.

When Suzy was a ghost,
a ghost Suzy was,
she went oo oo oo-oo-oo,
oo oo oo oo oo-oo-oo.

When Suzy was an angel,
an angel Suzy was,
she went amen amen amen
start again.

●

Toi-toi

Related by a teacher in Western Cape,
South Africa, 1986

A 6-year-old boy said to me 'Just watch me jump. I jump very high, eh?' I said to him 'Ja', but I wasn't paying any particular interest and he kept on insisting that I should watch how he jumps. And I said to him 'But why are you insisting?' He says 'One has to jump high because prison walls are high.' I said to him 'Now, do you think you are going to prison?' He said to me 'Yes, I'm going to prison.' I said to him 'Why?' He said 'Because I'm a comrade, and tell the children to come outside. I tell the teacher I'm going to the toilet and I call the children out and I teach them to toi-toi (do the freedom dance) so they're going to put me in prison.'

•

I warned you

A story related by a boy aged nine,
London, 1989

Three men were walking along when they came to a cave. One of them went in and saw a piece of toast in there. He went to pick it up when he heard this voice say:

I'M THE GHOST
THAT GUARDS THE TOAST

so the man ran out, and he says to the others,
'Don't go in there, there's a ghost in there.'
But the second man says, 'I ain't scared, I'm going in.'

So he goes in and he sees the piece of toast and he goes
to pick it up when he hears the voice:

I'M THE GHOST
THAT GUARDS THE TOAST

so the man ran out and he says to the third man,
'Don't go in there, there's a ghost in there.'
But the third man says, 'I ain't scared, I'm going in.'

So he goes in and he sees the piece of toast and he
thinks, I ain't bothered, and he grabbed it and stuffed
it in his mouth and ate it all up. And the voice called
out:

I WARNED YOU ONCE
I WARNED YOU TWICE
I WIPE MY BUM
ON EVERY SLICE.

Which should our priority be – to keep our promises to
the bankers or our promise to look after hungry children?
. . . We will not accept that it is necessary to starve children
in order to pay interest on debts to people who live in
luxury.

Anuradha Vittachi, *Stolen Childhood*

Punk boy

Poem by Basid, aged ten,
Bethnal Green, London, 1989

Punk boy is snatching Abul's stereo,
Abul is crying.
Will that punk boy murder Abul with his sharp knife?

'I don't care if you cry.
If you cry really loudly
I will murder you.' says the boy.

I say to Abul in Bengali:
'Handis na anniler fuiy marylybo.'
(Don't cry or that boy will murder us.)

We can't go home.
I'm scared.

●

The fib

A journalist reports on lying

The mother of one seven-year-old recalls: 'We went into the shop next to Tom's school to get things for tea. As we were walking down the street Tom said: "In that shop it would be very easy for chewing gum to fall into your pocket." I guessed at once he had stolen some but I didn't accuse him, I said. "I imagine it would be easy. But if it happened, the right thing would be to put the gum back because otherwise it could look like stealing." Tom then produced the gum, told me that it had fallen into his pocket and he wanted to take it back. I agreed

this was a good idea in a way I hoped would let him know I
knew he was lying, but without actually having to accuse him.'

In 1990 there were 170 million malnourished children in
the world.

In the same year 142 million children were born; 68 per
cent will be dead before the age of 16. That breaks down
into 3 per cent from the industrialized world and 65 per
cent from the developing world.

UNICEF, *The State of the World's Children*

. . . and when he . . .

Samantha, Justine and Colette discuss
Honey, I Shrunk the Kids, London, 1993

Samantha: . . . And then, and they went up the room and
something happened and they SHRUNK and then
the man mashed up the machine and they were
saying and then he swept down and they managed
to get a knife and cut it, cut something through the
blag – black bag and then they um the grass was
HORRIBLE and there was this ANT and it was
SLIMY [ergh!] [*laughter*], it was all slimy and it
showed really big on the camera and it was HOR-
RIBLE and me and my cousin every time we saw it

we would cover our faces cause it was all DISGUST-
ING [*laughing*] and they were friends with the ant and
they were saying [*imitates:*] 'He haw, he haw!'.
Cause it was running. [Yeah!] and they found this
little piece, little piece of um Lego and because they
didn't I mean um there was this man and he was
smoking and wasn't supposed to be smoking and
he threw it on the grass [*laughter*] and then and then
it went BUMPH and then and this – the boy who hit
the ball into the thing he – he got this stick and he
lit a fire so that they could all see where they were
going and they saw this Lego – the little boy's Lego
that [and they slept in it.

Justine: [The one that had been left on the grass

Samantha: And then and the and the girl was sleeping in the
Lego and the boy said 'Ah, I don't mind'. Cause he
fell in love with her [*sentimental tone:*] and then they
kissed [*laughs*]. They were kissing and then this
SCORPION came [Yeah!] and the ant and the
scorpion had a fight and it [died

Justine: [and the ant died cause
the scorpion killed it.

Samantha: It was sad.

Justine: But I don't know how the scorpion got there.
Because it can only get there because you can only
get them like in the jungle.

Samantha: Yeah [*concurring*] in the seaside [and all the mud was
on it and the dad was looking for it and then the
water

Justine: [[. . .]

Samantha: And then it was all [. . .] and then the girl got
drowned in this mud stuff [yeah!] [and the boy
saved her!

Justine: [in the mud.

Samantha: And because he saved her that's why they were
               kissing and but it was good [and at the end they
               turned into real people.
Justine: [[. . .]
Samantha: And the man who didn't like the other man [it was
               SO FUNNY [*laughing*]
Justine: [and he
               got the machine =
Samantha: = and he was sitting on this thing and um the boy
               pressed this thing and then they [. . .] and they
               nearly fell off the chair again like this [*laughing*], and
               then he done it again didn't he?
Justine: Yeah and there was this machine and they made the
               chicken go really big [on the table
Colette: [Yeah, what about the breakfast
               bit?
Justine: Yeah.
Samantha: And, and – oh yeah! And the dog found them so he
               put them on a tongue alright and then he put them
               on a table and and and um the little boy went into
               the cereal the boy was eating and he went =
Justine: = No, the man saw it

●

The pregnancy

A newspaper report

Even though I fell pregnant for my first child at 13, I was
actually planning to become pregnant. To this day I still haven't
understood why I wanted to have a baby so much. Sometimes I
wonder if it was due to my upbringing, as I watched my father

walk out of the door when I was about six years old and I am forever having arguments with my mother. Perhaps I wanted a baby to love in the way that I felt I had not been.

I met the father of my two children at my 13th birthday party. I didn't know him and he was not invited, but a couple of boys that live near me who I hadn't invited brought him along when they gatecrashed. During the party I was informed by a friend that Adam (my boyfriend) liked me. I didn't take much notice of this though, as I was too busy celebrating my birthday.

When the party was over, me and Adam, who was 15 then, started talking. He asked me out but I refused, but all of the following day he was hanging around pestering me, so after two days I accepted and have been with him ever since.

I had been seeing Adam for two months when I slept with him. Unlike a lot of teenage girls I was not pressurized. Neither of us had any past sexual experience and we weren't using any contraceptives. Three months later I fell pregnant. When I told Adam, he was quite happy. We spoke about the consequences of having a child whilst we were both so young and Adam's sister (a mother of four) had a chat with us and explained the realities of bringing up a baby.

Me and Adam decided that an abortion was not what we wanted. We wanted to keep this baby and give it as good a life as possible. Adam helped me a lot moneywise. He got a small cleaning job and everything he earned we would spend on things we would need for our baby.

When I told my mum that I was pregnant she was shocked but very supportive. She asked me to go home and live with her again. I did. My dad insisted I have an abortion, and I insisted that I would not. He was very upset and I don't blame him. It is not an everyday thing for your 13-year-old daughter to get pregnant. Anyway, after a few weeks my dad did finally accept that I was going to continue with my pregnancy.

In Britain more than 7,000 children a year are hurt so badly
by their parents that they need doctors.

Caroline Moorhead, ed., *Betrayal*

A Year's Headlines

Girl, aged thirteen, in Sarajevo, February 1993

I was standing beside a boy who was killed. I saw him being injured and dropping down. Then his head fell off.

Guardian, 27 February 1993

Rosalind Coward on 'Why little angels become monsters'

All the evidence is that the crisis around children is really a crisis about ourselves. We slide from extolling childhood innocence to calling for the devils to be incarcerated in sin bins because that's how we feel about ourselves. We are anxious about our capacity to keep our children 'good' because we doubt our own ability to create and sustain a 'good' society. We want the best but we feel we are failing. We have lost a sense of potency as parents and we are blaming children for our excesses.

Observer, 28 March 1993

Timothy Ross in Bogotá

The United Nations Children's Fund announced that, although 1,000 minors are murdered annually in Brazil, in Colombia – with a quarter of the population – twice as many die violently every year.

Most of the killings are carried out by self-proclaimed clean-up groups.

Guardian, 13 August 1993

Derek Brown reporting from Delhi

Leading a small but raucous demonstration in the heart of Delhi were nine of the carpet children liberated on Tuesday from inhuman conditions in the village of Tilthi, in Uttar Pradesh state . . . Uday and the other children carried makeshift banners asking 'Why are we slaves?' and declaring: 'Threds [sic] of carpets are chains of our slavery.'

Guardian, 21 September 1993

Dr Michael Fitzpatrick on 'Who's Really Bad?'

The result of more than five years of public concern about child abuse is the increase in state power and authority over family life. This does nothing to help abused children, but it reinforces the grip of a decadent establishment over a demoralised society.

Living Marxism, October 1993

Professor Richard Whitfield, Honorary Chairman of the National Family Trust

We have disenfranchised our young, both in the labour market and in the nurture to which they are entitled. Emotional neglect is worse than child labour, if labour means sweeping stations, doing paid jobs for the community, extending the concept of the paper round. That would be better for children than isolation at home, or trailing after a neighbourhood yob culture.

Quoted in *Independent on Sunday*, 31 October 1993

Fiona Smith speaking at the annual conference of the
Institute of British Geographers, Nottingham, 1994

Approximately a fifth of all five-to-10-year-olds are now left alone after school or in the holidays because both parents are at work. That is some 800,000 children, and unless action on childcare is taken rapidly the figure will only get worse.

Guardian, 6 January 1994

Are British children a

Boy drives drunk father home

AN AUSTRALIAN man has been charged after letting his 11-year-old son drive him home when he realised he was too drunk.

Boy, 9, admits spate of thefts

Boy, 4, found

Each day in northern Iraq, Kurdish children are killed and maimed by the legacy of a war that ended five years ago. For the sake of a few Iraqi dinars, they risk their lives stripping ammunition which was abandoned by the Iraqi army after the war against Iran. Recently, six children were blown to bits while attempting to remove fuses from Iraqi shells in order to extract a handful of aluminium.

ublic nuisance?

Boy, 5, thrown on to bonfire

hanged with tie after telling-off

43 per cent of children between the ages of 10 and 16 already have a job — 74 per cent of which are illegal. A quarter of them earn less than £1 an hour, and half work either before 7am or after 7pm. Small wonder that more than a third suffer accidents at work (including cuts, burns and broken bones).

Mortars kill children at Bosnia school

3m children 'living below poverty line'

US parents agonise over children's divorces

Quarter of under-

Youth crushed to death

John Farrington, 13, of Heckfield, Hampshire, was crushed to death yesterday by a trailer which became detached from a tractor near Yateley.

Cold-blooded killer, 12, sentenced to 25 years

Why the boys killed Daddy

Expulsion will leave six children alone

CONDOM vending machines could be installed in schools in the Highlands of Scotland after a survey showed that almost a fifth of pupils had had sexual intercourse by the age of 13.

The survey of more than 600 schoolchildren, carried out by the Highland Health Board, found that nearly 40 per cent had had sex by the time they reached the fourth year of school.

A quarter did not use contraceptives because they were too embarrassed to buy them in their home towns.

11s drink alcohol

BOY KILLED BY THREE TEASPOONS OF SALT

Acknowledgements

The publishers would like to thank the following for permission to reprint copyright extracts:

Saïd Aburish: to I. B. Tauris & Co. Ltd, London, for *Children of Bethany: The Story of a Palestinian Family*

Philippe Ariès: to the Estate of the author, the translator, and Random House UK Ltd, for *Centuries of Childhood* (Jonathan Cape Ltd)

Basid: to Frank Tarrant and John Scurr School, London, for 'Punk Boy' from *I Think I'm Bad, I Know I'm Bad*

Victoria Brittain and Abdul S. Minty, eds.: to Mayibuye Centre, University of the Western Cape, for *Children of Resistance* (Kliptown Books)

David Buckingham: to Taylor & Francis Publishers for *Children Talking Television*

John Burnett: to Routledge Ltd for *Destiny Obscure*

H. E. Butler, ed. and trans.: to Random House UK Ltd for *The Autobiography of Giraldus Cambrensis* (Jonathan Cape Ltd)

Jung Chang: to Harper Collins Publishers Ltd for *Wild Swans: Three Daughters of China*

Sharon Cheeks: to National Exhibition of Children's Art, London, for 'S-t-r-e-t-c-h-i-n-g' from *The Kingfisher Book of Children's Poetry*, ed. Michael Rosen

C. G. Coulton: to Cambridge University Press for *Life in the Middle Ages*

Zelda D'Aprano: to the author for *Zelda: The Becoming of a Woman* (Spinifex Press)

Walter de la Mare: to The Literary Trustees of Walter de la Mare, and The Society of Authors as their representative, for *Early One Morning in the Spring*

Gwyn Dow and June Factor, eds.: to Penguin Books Australia Ltd for *Australian Childhood*

Mihi Edwards: to Penguin Books (NZ) Ltd for *Mihipeka: Early Years*

Mark Golden: to Johns Hopkins University Press for *Children and Childhood in Classical Athens*

Guardian: to Syndication Department for newspaper articles, reports and letters

John Hegley: to Peters Fraser & Dunlop Group Ltd and Methuen, London, for 'Greed' from *Five Sugars Please*

Martin Hoyles: to Pluto Press for *The Politics of Childhood*

Stephen Humphries: to Blackwell Publishers for *Hooligans or Rebels?: An Oral History of Working Class Childhood and Youth 1889–1939*

Stephen Humphries and Pamela Gordon: to Northcote House Publishers for *Out of Sight*

Independent: to Syndication Department for poems, letter and articles

Susan Isaacs: to Routledge & Kegan Paul for *Social Development in Young Children* and *The Intellectual Growth of Young Children*

David Jackson: to the collator (David Jackson) and children of Toot Hill Comprehensive School, Bingham, Nottinghamshire, for 'Parents' irritating sayings'

R. D. Laing: to Penguin Books Ltd and the R. D. Laing Estate for *Conversations with Children*. Copyright © R. D. Laing, 1978

Margaret Lane: to Frederick Warne & Co. for *The Tale of Beatrix Potter: A Biography*. Copyright © Frederick Warne & Co., 1946

Miriam Lichtheim: to University of California Press for *Ancient Egyptian Literature*. Three volumes. Copyright © 1973–1980 Regents of the University of California

Janet McCalman: to Melbourne University Press for *Struggletown: Public and Private Life in Richmond 1900–1965*

Caroline Moorhead: to Random House UK Ltd for *Betrayal* (Barrie & Jenkins)

Oodgeroo Noonuccal: to Angus & Robertson, a division of HarperCollins Publishers (Australia) Pty Ltd, for *Stradbroke Dreamtime*

Iona Opie: to Oxford University Press for *The People in the Playground*. Copyright © Iona Opie, 1993

Vivian Gussin Paley: to Harvard University Press for *Wally's Stories*. Copyright © 1981 by the President and Fellows of Harvard College; to University of Chicago Press for *Bad Guys Don't Have Birthdays*

Dorothy Scannell: to the author for *Mother Knew Best*, Macmillan

Harold Silver: to Routledge Ltd for *Education of the Poor*

Michael Swanton, trans.: to Everyman's Library Ltd for *Anglo-Saxon Prose*

Junichiro Tanizaki: to Kodansha International for *Childhood Years: A Memoir*. English translation copyright © 1988 by Kodansha International

Sunday Times: to Syndication Department for 'Signs of the times' (5/12/ 93), and 'Happy family is a thing of the past' by Peter Kellner (29/8/93). Copyright © Times Newspapers Ltd, 1993

Anuradha Vittachi: to Blackwell Publishers for *Stolen Childhood*

Martha Wolfenstein: to The Free Press, an imprint of Simon & Schuster, for *Children's Humor: A Psychological Study*. Copyright © 1954 by The Free Press; copyright renewed 1982 by Eugene Victor Wolfenstein

Every effort has been made to contact copyright holders. The publishers will be glad to rectify, in future editions, any omissions brought to their notice.

References

p. 3

Dad knows best: Rosalind M. and Jac J. Janssen, *Growing Up in Ancient Egypt*, Rubicon Press, 1990

Pupil to teacher: Rosalind M. and Jac J. Janssen, *Growing Up in Ancient Egypt*, Rubicon Press, 1990

Grave message: Miriam Lichtheim, *Ancient Egyptian Literature. Volume III: The Late Period*, University of California Press, 1980

p. 4

What to do with boys: Barry S. Strauss, *Fathers and Sons in Athens*, Routledge, 1993

p. 5

Girls play 'The Tortoise': Mark Golden, *Children and Childhood in Classical Athens*, Johns Hopkins Press, 1990

Iphis speaks: Mark Golden, *Children and Childhood in Classical Athens*, Johns Hopkins Press, 1990

p. 6

Creon speaks: Mark Golden, *Children and Childhood in Classical Athens*, Johns Hopkins Press, 1990

Decline in standards: Helen Handley and Andra Samelson, eds., *Childhood*, Robert Hale, 1990

Bedwetting explained: Lloyd de Mause, *The History of Childhood*, Bellew Publishing, 1991

p. 7

A brave girl: Thomas Wiedemann, *Adults and Children in the Roman Empire*, Routledge, 1989

The beastly foreigners: Lloyd de Mause, *The History of Childhood*, Bellew Publishing, 1991

p. 8

Castration not complex: Lloyd de Mause, *The History of Childhood*, Bellew Publishing, 1991

Romans on childhood: Thomas Wiedemann, *Adults and Children in the Roman Empire*, Routledge, 1989

p. 9

Mutilating children for freak shows: Lloyd de Mause, *The History of Childhood*, Bellew Publishing, 1991

Vipstanus Messalla complains: John K. Evans, *War, Women and Children in Ancient Rome*, Routledge, 1991

p. 10

Ducks and drakes: John K. Evans, *War, Women and Children in Ancient Rome*, Routledge, 1991

Dear Dad . . .: Walter de la Mare, *Early One Morning in the Spring*, Faber & Faber, 1949

p. 11

Naughty: Penelope Hughes-Hallett, *Childhood*, Collins, 1988

Granddad's words of wisdom: Thomas Wiedemann, *Adults and Children in the Roman Empire*, Routledge, 1989

p. 12

Boy-kings are a pain: Thomas Wiedemann, *Adults and Children in the Roman Empire*, Routledge, 1989

At the school for monks: Michael Swanton, translator, *Anglo-Saxon Prose*, Everyman, 1993

p. 14

In the sand-pit: W. O. Hassall, *They Saw it Happen*, Basil Blackwell, 1957

Fear of candles: Richard Kay, *Medieval Anecdotes*, Broadview Press, 1988

p. 15

Are they not human?: G. G. Coulton, *Life in the Middle Ages*, Cambridge University Press, 1967

p. 17

She loves me, she loves me not ...: Alice Morse Earle, *Child Life in Colonial Days*, 1899

Equality some way off: Shulamith Shahar, *Childhood in the Middle Ages*, Routledge, 1990

Justice: Shulamith Shahar, *Childhood in the Middle Ages*, Routledge, 1990

p. 18

Body contact in the monastery: G. G. Coulton, *Life in the Middle Ages*, Cambridge University Press, 1967

Medieval romping: G. G. Coulton, *Life in the Middle Ages*, Cambridge University Press, 1967

p. 20

A bit young for the job: G. G. Coulton, *Life in the Middle Ages*, Cambridge University Press, 1967

A separation before execution: Shulamith Shahar, *Childhood in the Middle Ages*, Routledge, 1990

p. 21

Upsetting the order: Martin Hoyles, *The Politics of Childhood*, Pluto Press

The quaynte games of a wanton chylde: Susan Miles, ed., *Childhood in Verse and Prose*, Oxford University Press, 1923

p. 22

Don't pick your nose: Iona and Peter Opie, *The Oxford Book of Children's Verse*, Oxford University Press, 1973

p. 23

When my Dad was a boy ...: Lloyd de Mause, *The History of Childhood*, Bellew Publishing, 1991

Me and my mates: Alice Morse Earle, *Child Life in Colonial Days*, 1899

p. 24

A moan: Lloyd de Mause, *The History of Childhood*, Bellew Publishing, 1991

Please can I go to the . . .: Keith Thomas, *Children in Early Modern England*, quoted in Julia Avery and Gillian Briggs, eds., *Children and Their Books*, Oxford University Press, 1989

p. 25

Hobby-horse: D. M. Stuart, *The Girl Through the Ages*, George Harrap & Co. Ltd, 1933

How to be mannerly: Iona and Peter Opie, *The Oxford Book of Children's Verse*, Oxford University Press, 1973

p. 26

Don't throw your bones on the floor: Iona and Peter Opie, *The Oxford Book of Children's Verse*, Oxford University Press, 1973

p. 28

The horrible English: Lloyd de Mause, *The History of Childhood*, Bellew Publishing, 1991

p. 29

Home tuition: Lloyd de Mause, *The History of Childhood*, Bellew Publishing, 1991

Dirty bits: Philippe Ariès, *Centuries of Childhood*, Librairie Plon, 1960; Jonathan Cape, 1962; Penguin Books Ltd, 1973

p. 30

Beat him: Anita Schorsch, *Images of Childhood*, Mayflower, New York, 1979

I hate scole: David Wright, ed., *Penguin Book of Everyday Verse*, Penguin Books Ltd, 1983

p. 32

Go to work: Walter de la Mare, *Early One Morning in the Spring*, Faber & Faber, 1949

No more unfittinge festivals: W. Carew Hazlitt, *Dictionary of Faith and Folklore*, [n.d.]

p. 34

A gentle schoolmaster: D. M. Stuart, *The Girl Through the Ages*, George Harrap & Co. Ltd, 1933

Bunking off: Gillian Avery and Julia Briggs, eds., *Children and Their Books*, Oxford University Press, 1989

p. 35

Child marriage: first night problems: F. J. Furnivall, *Child-Marriages, Divorces etc.*, 1897

Child marriage: four in the bed: F. J. Furnivall, *Child-Marriages, Divorces etc.*, 1897

p. 36

Child marriage: too young to agree: F. J. Furnivall, *Child-Marriages, Divorces etc.*, 1897

We hate maths: Alice Morse Earle, *Child Life in Colonial Days*, 1899

p. 37

The kids aren't worth much: Anita Schorsch, *Images of Childhood*, Mayflower, New York, 1979

Slippery slope: Gillian Avery and Julia Briggs, eds., *Children and Their Books*, Oxford University Press, 1989

Wool-sorters useful: Lloyd de Mause, *The History of Childhood*, Bellew Publishing, 1991

p. 38

Cock of the walk: Philippe Ariès, *Centuries of Childhood*, Random House UK Ltd (Jonathan Cape Ltd, 1962)

p. 40

Royal toys: Anita Schorsch, *Images of Childhood*, Mayflower, New York, 1979

Be kynd, Dad: Walter de la Mare, *Early One Morning in the Spring*, Faber & Faber, 1949

p. 41

Beginnings: Lloyd de Mause, *The History of Childhood*, Bellew Publishing, 1991

Girls can: Walter de la Mare, *Early One Morning in the Spring*, Faber & Faber, 1949

p. 42

Light blue touch paper ...: Keith Thomas, *Children in Early Modern England*, quoted in Gillian Avery and Julia Briggs, eds., *Children and Their Books*, Oxford University Press, 1989

p. 43

Beasts: Gillian Avery and Julia Briggs, eds., *Children and Their Books*, Oxford University Press, 1989

Kindergarten Latin: Linda A. Pollock, *Forgotten Children: Parent–Child Relations from 1500–1900*, Cambridge University Press, 1983

p. 44

A holy twelve-year-old: Alice Morse Earle, *Child Life in Colonial Days*, 1899

Ship 'em off: Anita Schorsch, *Images of Childhood*, Mayflower, New York, 1979

p. 45

Free of reason: Lloyd de Mause, *The History of Childhood*, Bellew Publishing, 1991

Of the boy and the butterfly: Iona and Peter Opie, *The Oxford Book of Children's Verse*, Oxford University Press, 1973

p. 46

Sparing the rod: Linda A. Pollock, *Forgotten Children: Parent–Child Relations from 1500–1900*, Cambridge University Press, 1983

p. 47

Four years without thrashing: Lloyd de Mause, *The History of Childhood*, Bellew Publishing, 1991

Girls and dolls: Gillian Avery and Julia Briggs, eds., *Children and Their Books*, Oxford University Press, 1989

p. 48

Let's get giddy: Gillian Avery and Julia Briggs, eds., *Children and Their Books*, Oxford University Press, 1989

Rudeness: Gillian Avery and Julia Briggs, eds., *Children and Their Books*, Oxford University Press, 1989

A hoyting girl: Walter de la Mare, *Early One Morning in the Spring*, Faber & Faber, 1949

p. 49

Breeching little ffrank: Alice Morse Earle, *Child Life in Colonial Days*, 1899

p. 50

The death of Papa: Susan Miles, ed., *Childhood in Verse and Prose*, Oxford University Press, 1923

p. 51

Sam worried: Linda A. Pollock, *Forgotten Children*, Cambridge University Press, 1983

John, Mary, Betty, Tom and William: Gillian Avery and Julia Briggs, eds., *Children and Their Books*, Oxford University Press, 1989

p. 52

Listen, Katy . . .: Alice Morse Earle, *Child Life in Colonial Days*, 1899

p. 53

God doesn't like vain sports: Anita Schorsch, *Images of Childhood*, Mayflower, New York, 1979

Nothing fancy at the Wesleys: Anita Schorsch, *Images of Childhood*, Mayflower, New York, 1979

p. 54

At the temporary store for bodies in the graveyard: Lloyd de Mause, *The History of Childhood*, Bellew Publishing, 1991

It's my book: Alice Morse Earle, *Child Life in Colonial Days*, 1899

p. 55

Small ad.: I. Stickland, *The Voices of the Children*, Basil Blackwell, 1973

Alex, Bob and wot I think: Gillian Avery and Julia Briggs, eds., *Children and Their Books*, Oxford University Press, 1989

. . . and don't forget the . . .: Gillian Avery and Julia Briggs, eds., *Children and Their Books*, Oxford University Press, 1989

p. 56

Against quarrelling and fighting: Isaac Watts, *Divine Songs Attempted in Easy Language for the Use of Children*, 1715

p. 57

Grandpa speaks: Lloyd de Mause, *The History of Childhood*, Bellew Publishing, 1991

Grown up: Alice Morse Earle, *Child Life in Colonial Days*, 1899

p. 58

Dear Mum: Gillian Avery and Julia Briggs, eds., *Children and Their Books*, Oxford University Press, 1989

How to be nice: Anita Schorsch, *Images of Childhood*, Mayflower, New York, 1979

p. 59

The drugs solution for children: I. Stickland, *The Voices of the Children*, Basil Blackwell, 1973

Dirty books: Gillian Avery and Julia Briggs, *Children and Their Books*, Oxford University Press, 1989

p. 60

Dear Dad: Alice Morse Earle, *Child Life in Colonial Days*, 1899

Captured: Abraham Chapman, ed., *Steal Away*, Ernest Benn Ltd, 1973; Paul Edwards, ed., *Equiano's Travels*, Heinemann, 1967

p. 63

Spoilt American kids: Anita Schorsch, *Images of Childhood*, Mayflower, New York, 1979

p. 64

The non-believer: Linda A. Pollock, *Forgotten Children*, Cambridge University Press, 1983

All dressed up: Alice Morse Earle, *Child Life in Colonial Days*, 1899

p. 65

Trying to be diligent: Alice Morse Earle, *Child Life in Colonial Days*, 1899

p. 66

The dreamer: Walter de la Mare, *Early One Morning in the Spring*, Faber & Faber, 1949

p. 67

An old Scots remedy: Walter de la Mare, *Early One Morning in the Spring*, Faber & Faber, 1949

p. 68

The school dungeons: Susan Miles, ed., *Childhood in Verse and Prose*, Oxford University Press, 1923

p. 69

A home entertainment: Walter de la Mare, *Early One Morning in the Spring*, Faber & Faber, 1949

Every man his place in life: Anita Schorsch, *Images of Childhood*, Mayflower, New York, 1979

p. 70

National order: Hugh Cunningham, *The Children of the Poor*, Blackwell, 1991

The problem with slaves: Cited in Mark Golden, *Children and Childhood in Classical Athens*, Johns Hopkins Press, 1990

p. 71

Good and bad: Alice Morse Earle, *Child Life in Colonial Days*, 1899

p. 73

Dad as a boy: Mary Sewell, *Reminiscences*, 1882

p. 74

An educational sandhill: Susan Miles, ed., *Childhood in Verse and Prose*, Oxford University Press, 1923

p. 75

A vision: Walter de la Mare, *Early One Morning in the Spring*, Faber & Faber, 1949

Keep your clothes on: Anita Schorsch, *Images of Childhood*, Mayflower, New York, 1979

p. 77

Goodbye, little bastard: Anita Schorsch, *Images of Childhood*, Mayflower, New York, 1979

Curing prostitution in the colony: Gwyn Dow and June Factor, eds., *Australian Childhood*, Penguin Books Australia Ltd, 1991

p. 78

Keep the clothes decent: Anita Schorsch, *Images of Childhood*, Mayflower, New York, 1979

A less than useful wall: Walter de la Mare, *Early One Morning in the Spring*, Faber & Faber, 1949

p. 79

Scenes of our childhood: Michael Rosen, ed., *The World of Poetry*, Kingfisher, 1991

p. 81

A delightful dawdle: Linda A. Pollock, *Forgotten Children: Parent–Child Relationships from 1500–1900*, Cambridge University Press, 1983

A little devil: Linda A. Pollock, *Forgotten Children: Parent–Child Relationships from 1500–1900*, Cambridge University Press, 1983

p. 82

A good teacher: Mary Sewell, *Reminiscences*, 1882

p. 83

Memories and feelings: Walter de la Mare, *Early One Morning in the Spring*, Faber & Faber, 1949; ibid.; Susan Miles, ed., *Childhood in Verse and Prose*, Oxford University Press, 1923

p. 84

Busy day: Pamela and Harold Silver, *The Education of the Poor*, Routledge & Kegan Paul, 1974

p. 85

Slave-girl: Abraham Chapman, ed., *Steal Away*, Ernest Benn Ltd, 1973

p. 87

A friendly word of advice: Walter de la Mare, *Early One Morning in the Spring*, Faber & Faber, 1949

Great writer's secret love: Helen Handley and Andra Samelson, *Childhood*, Robert Hale, 1990

Female tasks: Eileen Simpson, *Orphans*, Weidenfeld & Nicolson, 1987

p. 88

Making a living: John Burnett, *Destiny Obscure*, Routledge Ltd

p. 89

Sufficient possessions: Walter de la Mare, *Early One Morning in the Spring*, Faber & Faber, 1949

p. 90

The road-mender's family: I. Stickland, *The Voices of the Children*, Basil Blackwell, 1973

A heavy punishment: E. Royston Pike, ed., *Human Documents of the Industrial Revolution in Britain*, George Allen & Unwin, 1966

p. 91

Funny uniform: Walter de la Mare, *Early One Morning in the Spring*, Faber & Faber, 1949

p. 92

A scientist: Walter de la Mare, *Early One Morning in the Spring*, Faber & Faber, 1949

p. 93

Guilt: John Burnett, *Destiny Obscure*, Routledge Ltd

p. 94

A twelve-year-old convict: Gwyn Dow and June Factor, eds., *Australian Childhood*, Penguin Books Australia Ltd, 1991

p. 95

A coal-miner: E. Royston Pike, ed., *Human Documents of the Industrial Revolution in Britain*, George Allen & Unwin, 1966

Pranks: Walter de la Mare, *Early One Morning in the Spring*, Faber & Faber, 1949

p. 96

A first memory: Edmund Gosse, *Father and Son*, Heinemann, 1907

The collector: Walter de la Mare, *Early One Morning in the Spring*, Faber & Faber, 1949

p. 97

A real sin: Walter de la Mare, *Early One Morning in the Spring*, Faber & Faber, 1949

A treasure island: Susan Miles, ed., *Childhood in Verse and Prose*, Oxford University Press., 1923

p. 98

Backstreet care: Henry Mayhew, *London Labour and the London Poor*, 1861

p. 99

Ducking and diving: Henry Mayhew, *London Labour and the London Poor*, 1861

p. 100

Excuses, excuses: Pamela and Harold Silver, *The Education of the Poor*, Routledge & Kegan Paul, 1974

p. 101

Bug-lore: Alice Morse Earle, *Child Life in Colonial Days*, 1899

p. 102

Beloved children: Walter de la Mare, *Early One Morning in the Spring*, Faber & Faber, 1949

Eton beating: I. Stickland, *The Voices of the Children*, Basil Blackwell, 1973

p. 103

A good education: Margaret Lane, *The Tale of Beatrix Potter*, Warne, 1946

p. 104

Many happy hours: Anita Schorsch, *Images of Childhood*, Mayflower, New York, 1979

He learned the boy: Stephen Humphries, *Hooligans or Rebels?*, Blackwell, 1981

p. 105

A frightening king: Junichiro Tanizaki, *Childhood Years: A Memoir*, Kodansha International Ltd

p. 106

A silly little girl: I. Stickland, *The Voices of the Children*, Basil Blackwell, 1973

A punishment: Karl Shaw, *Gross*, Virgin, 1993

p. 107

The man's way: I. Stickland, *The Voices of the Children*, Basil Blackwell, 1973

What they say: William Canton, ed., *Children's Sayings*, 1900

p. 108

The bedroom: Extracted in John Burnett, *Destiny Obscure*, Routledge Ltd

Family life: Extracted in John Burnett, *Destiny Obscure*, Routledge Ltd

p. 110

Not knowing Noah: Gwyn Dow and June Factor, eds., *Australian Childhood*, Penguin Books Australia Ltd, 1991

A warm new sensation: Walter de la Mare, *Early One Morning in the Spring*, Faber & Faber, 1949

p. 111

Song: Dudley Kidd, *Savage Childhood* [sic], Adam and Charles Black, 1906

The tooth-bird: Dudley Kidd, *Savage Childhood* [sic], Adam and Charles Black, 1906

p. 112

Zulu backslang: Dudley Kidd, *Savage Childhood* [sic], Adam and Charles Black, 1906

Australian cowboy: from *The Beckoning Horizon*, 1983, in Gwyn Dow and June Factor, eds., *Australian Childhood*, Penguin Books Australia Ltd, 1991

p. 113

Kangaroo hunter: *Nothing to Spare: Recollections of Australian Pioneering Women*, Penguin Books Ltd, 1981, quoted in Gwyn Dow and June Factor, eds., *Australian Childhood*, Penguin Books Australia Ltd, 1991

p. 114

An Edwardian childhood: Stephen Humphries, *Hooligans or Rebels?*, Blackwell, 1981

p. 116

Is it a dolly?: Stephen Potter, *Steps to Immaturity*, c. 1908, quoted in Penelope Hughes-Hallett, *Childhood*, Collins, 1988

p. 117

Out of bondage: Hsieh Ping-Ying, *Autobiography of a Chinese Girl*, Pandora, 1986

p. 120

Orphan Ivy: Stephen Humphries, *Hooligans or Rebels?: An Oral History of Working Class Childhood and Youth 1889–1939*, Blackwell Publishers, 1981

p. 121

Washday: John Burnett, *Destiny Obscure*, Routledge Ltd

Children's strike: Stephen Humphries, *Hooligans or Rebels?*, Blackwell, 1981

p. 123

She's in the Sally Army: Stephen Humphries, *Hooligans or Rebels?*, Blackwell, 1981

p. 124

Sudden death?: From Janet McCalman, *Struggletown: Public and Private Life in Richmond*, 1984, quoted in Gwyn Dow and June Factor, eds., *Australian Childhood*, Penguin Books Australia Ltd, 1991

The golf links: Anita Schorsch, *Images of Childhood*, Mayflower, New York, 1979

p. 125

Dealing with a truant: Stephen Humphries, Joanna Mack and Robert Perks, *A Century of Childhood*, Channel 4 and Sidgwick & Jackson, 1988

p. 126

Bottom: Extracted in John Burnett, *Destiny Obscure*, Routledge Ltd

p. 127

Absolute silence: Stephen Humphries and Pamela Gordon, *Out of Sight*, Channel 4/Northcote House, 1992

Polio: Stephen Humphries and Pamela Gordon, *Out of Sight*, Channel 4/Northcote House, 1992

p. 128

An alternative view: Stephen Humphries, *Hooligans or Rebels?*, Blackwell, 1981

p. 129

The Brownies: From *Girl Guides: A Handbook for Guidelets, Guides, Senior Guides and Guiders*, The Guide Association, 1918

p. 131

Finding out about steam: Dorothy Scannell, *Mother Knew Best: An East End Childhood*, Macmillan, 1974

Afraid of passing exams: Stephen Humphries, *Hooligans or Rebels?*, Blackwell, 1981

p. 133

The hiring fair: Stephen Humphries, Joanna Mack and Robert Perks, *A Century of Childhood*, Channel 4 and Sidgwick & Jackson, 1988

p. 134

On an Aboriginal penal settlement: Gwyn Dow and June Factor, eds., *Australian Childhood*, Penguin Books Australia Ltd, 1991

p. 135

A Maori girl's first day at school: From *Mihipeka: Early Years* in Witi

Ihimaera, ed., *Te Ao Mārama: Contemporary Maori Writing*, vol. 1, Reed Books (New Zealand), 1992

Sex education: Stephen Humphries, Joanna Mack, Robert Perks, *A Century of Childhood*, Channel 4 and Sidgwick & Jackson, 1988

p. 136

Why?: *The Jenny Lind Book of Children's Sayings*, collected by Helen C. Colman, Jarrold, 1927

More whys: Susan Isaacs, *Intellectual Growth in Young Children*, Routledge & Kegan Paul, 1930

p. 137

In New Guinea: Margaret Mead, *Growing Up in New Guinea*, Penguin Books Ltd, 1942

p. 139

Never for killing's sake: From Oodgeroo Noonuccal, *Stradbroke Dreamtime*, Angus & Robertson, HarperCollins Publishers (Australia) Pty, 1972, in Gwyn Dow and June Factor, eds., *Australian Childhood*, Penguin Books Australia Ltd, 1991

p. 142

Late again, boy: Stephen Humphries, *Hooligans or Rebels?*, Blackwell, 1981

p. 143

Cursed: Stephen Humphries and Pamela Gordon, *Out of Sight*, Channel 4/ Northcote House, 1992

p. 144

Bloody Jew: From Zelda D'Aprano, *Zelda: The Becoming of a Woman*, Spinifex Press, 1977, in Gwyn Dow and June Factor, eds., *Australian Childhood*, Penguin Books Australia Ltd, 1991

p. 145

Waiting for the baby: Susan Isaacs, *Social Development in Young Children*, Routledge & Kegan Paul, 1933

p. 148

Splints: Susan Isaacs, *Social Development in Young Children*, Routledge & Kegan Paul, 1933

p. 149

Not her fault: Susan Isaacs, *Social Development in Young Children*, Routledge & Kegan Paul, 1933

p. 150

A good game: Susan Isaacs, *Social Development in Young Children*, Routledge & Kegan Paul, 1933

Closely observed: Susan Isaacs, *Social Development in Young Children*, Routledge & Kegan Paul, 1933; and Susan Isaacs, *Intellectual Growth in Young Children*, Routledge & Kegan Paul, 1930

p. 153

The twins: Lucette Matalon Lagnado and Sheila Cohn Dekel, *Children of the Flames: Dr Josef Mengele and the Untold Story of the Twins of Auschwitz*, Pan, 1991

p. 155

The root of all evil: Walter de la Mare, *Early One Morning in the Spring*, Faber & Faber, 1949

p. 156

Circumcision: Saïd K. Aburish, *Children of Bethany: The Story of a Palestinian Family*, I. B. Tauris & Co. Ltd

p. 157

A joke: Martha Wolfenstein, *Children's Humor: A Psychological Study*, The Free Press, an imprint of Simon & Schuster

p. 158

An experiment: *Guardian*, 6 January 1994

p. 159

Revolutionary priorities: Jung Chang, *Wild Swans: Three Daughters of China*, HarperCollins, 1991

p. 160

My friend Billy: Michael Rosen, *Rude Rhymes*, Signet, 1992

Toast: Michael Rosen, ed., *The World of Poetry*, Kingfisher, 1991

p. 161

November 1975: R. D. Laing, *Conversations with Children*, Penguin Books Ltd, 1978

p. 162

Hunch Bunch: Michael Rosen, ed., *Rude Rhymes*, Signet, 1992

p. 163

Coming home: Michael Rosen, ed., *The World of Poetry*, Kingfisher, 1991

What parents say: Collated by David Jackson, Nottingham, 1978

p. 164

In the playground: Iona Opie, *People in the Playground*, Oxford University Press, 1978

p. 166

In the news: Iona Opie, *People in the Playground*, Oxford University Press, 1978

p. 167

Moving in: Michael Rosen, ed., *The World of Poetry*, Kingfisher, 1991

p. 168

Every morning: Michael Rosen, ed., *Kingfisher Book of Children's Poetry*, Kingfisher, 1985

Moon man: Vivian Gussin Paley, *Wally's Stories*, Harvard University Press, 1981

p. 170

Greed: A poem: John Hegley, *Five Sugars Please*, Methuen, 1993

p. 171

One of the wise men: Gary Younge, *Guardian*, 24 December 1993

Mam: Gitta Sereny, *Independent on Sunday*, 28 November 1993

p. 172

Sunday school teacher: Denys Thompson, ed., *Children as Poets*, Heinemann, 1972

p. 173

A hero: Vivian Gussin Paley, *Wally's Stories*, Harvard University Press, 1981

p. 174

Santa Claus: Vivian Gussin Paley, *Wally's Stories*, Harvard University Press, 1981

p. 176

The tooth gazelle: Vivian Gussin Paley, *Wally's Stories*, Harvard University Press, 1981

Getting the point: Vivian Gussin Paley, *Wally's Stories*, Harvard University Press, 1981

p. 177

Bad guy: Vivian Gussin Paley, *Bad Guys Don't Have Birthdays*, University of Chicago Press, 1988

p. 180

Skipping song: Michael Rosen, ed., *Rude Rhymes*, Signet, 1992

p. 181

S-t-r-e-t-c-h-i-n-g: Michael Rosen, ed., *The Kingfisher Book of Children's Poetry* (from *Cadbury's Second Selection of Children's Poetry*, by permission of Cadbury Schweppes), Kingfisher, 1985

My memories: Michael Rosen, *Did I Hear You Write?*, André Deutsch Ltd, 1989

p. 182

Understanding: Martin Hoyles and Susan Hemmings, eds., *More Valuable Than Gold* by Striking Miners' Children, Martin Hoyles, 1985

p. 183

Bed!: Michael Rosen, ed., *A Spider Bought a Bicycle*, Kingfisher, 1987

p. 184

Why?: Michael Rosen, ed., *A Spider Bought a Bicycle*, Kingfisher, 1987

Freedom: From *Two Dogs and Freedom* (The Open School, South Africa) reprinted in Michael Rosen, ed., *The World of Poetry*, Kingfisher, 1991

p. 185

Song: Michael Rosen, ed., *Rude Rhymes*, Signet, 1992

p. 188

Typically middle-class: Caroline Moorhead, ed., *Betrayal*, Barrie & Jenkins, 1989

I a boy one witch: Caroline Moorhead, ed., *Betrayal*, Barrie & Jenkins, 1989

p. 189

A dream: Michael Rosen, ed., *Did I Hear You Write?*, André Deutsch Ltd, 1989

p. 190

Detention: Caroline Moorhead, ed., *Betrayal*, Barrie & Jenkins, 1989

p. 191

On the streets: Caroline Moorhead, ed., *Betrayal*, Barrie & Jenkins, 1989

Song: Michael Rosen, ed., *Rude Rhymes*, Signet, 1992

p. 193

Toi toi: Victoria Brittain and Abdul S. Minty, *Children of Resistance*, Kliptown Books, 1988

p. 194

I warned you: Michael Rosen, ed., *Rude Rhymes*, Signet, 1992

p. 195

Punk boy: *I Think I'm Bad, I Know I'm Bad*. John Scurr Primary School, Cephas Street, London E1 4AX (Head Teacher: Frank Tarrant)

p. 196

The fib: Angela Neustatter, 'Telling the truth about lies', in *Independent on Sunday*, 10 May 1992

. . . and when he . . .: David Buckingham, *Children Talking Television*, Taylor & Francis Publishers

p. 198

The pregnancy: 'Alice' in the *Guardian*, 18 December 1993

References to 'boxes':

p. 33

Martin Hoyles, *The Politics of Childhood*, Pluto Press

p. 52

Anita Schorsch, *Images of Childhood*, Mayflower Books, New York, 1979

p. 76

Sir William Blackstone quoted in Walter de la Mare, *Early One Morning in the Spring*, Faber & Faber, 1949

p. 98

Eileen Simpson, *Orphans*, Weidenfeld & Nicolson, 1987

p. 103

Gillian Wagner, *Children of the Empire*, Weidenfeld & Nicolson, 1982

p. 109

Stephen Humphries, *Hooligans or Rebels?: An Oral History of Working Class Childhood and Youth 1889–1939*, Blackwell Publishers, 1981

p. 170

Trafficking in children from Brazil, 1980s, discussed in Caroline Blackwell, ed., *Betrayal*, Barrie & Jenkins, 1989

p. 186

Included in Anuradha Vittachi, *Stolen Childhood*, Blackwell Publishers

p. 195

Anuradha Vittachi, *Stolen Childhood*, Blackwell Publishers

p. 196

The State of the World's Children 1991, UNICEF, 1991

p. 200

Caroline Moorhead, ed., *Betrayal*, Barrie & Jenkins, 1989

READ MORE IN PENGUIN

In every corner of the world, on every subject under the sun, Penguin represents quality and variety – the very best in publishing today.

For complete information about books available from Penguin – including Puffins, Penguin Classics and Arkana – and how to order them, write to us at the appropriate address below. Please note that for copyright reasons the selection of books varies from country to country.

In the United Kingdom: Please write to *Dept. JC, Penguin Books Ltd, FREEPOST, West Drayton, Middlesex UB7 OBR.*

If you have any difficulty in obtaining a title, please send your order with the correct money, plus ten per cent for postage and packaging, to *PO Box No. 11, West Drayton, Middlesex UB7 OBR*

In the United States: Please write to *Consumer Sales, Penguin USA, P.O. Box 999, Dept. 17109, Bergenfield, New Jersey 07621-0120.* VISA and MasterCard holders call 1-800-253-6476 to order all Penguin titles

In Canada: Please write to *Penguin Books Canada Ltd, 10 Alcorn Avenue, Suite 300, Toronto, Ontario M4V 3B2*

In Australia: Please write to *Penguin Books Australia Ltd, P.O. Box 257, Ringwood, Victoria 3134*

In New Zealand: Please write to *Penguin Books (NZ) Ltd, Private Bag 102902, North Shore Mail Centre, Auckland 10*

In India: Please write to *Penguin Books India Pvt Ltd, 706 Eros Apartments, 56 Nehru Place, New Delhi 110 019*

In the Netherlands: Please write to *Penguin Books Netherlands bv, Postbus 3507, NL-1001 AH Amsterdam*

In Germany: Please write to *Penguin Books Deutschland GmbH, Metzlerstrasse 26, 60594 Frankfurt am Main*

In Spain: Please write to *Penguin Books S. A., Bravo Murillo 19, 1° B, 28015 Madrid*

In Italy: Please write to *Penguin Italia s.r.l., Via Felice Casati 20, I-20124 Milano*

In France: Please write to *Penguin France S. A., 17 rue Lejeune, F-31000 Toulouse*

In Japan: Please write to *Penguin Books Japan, Ishikiribashi Building, 2-5-4, Suido, Bunkyo-ku, Tokyo 112*

In Greece: Please write to *Penguin Hellas Ltd, Dimocritou 3, GR-106 71 Athens*

In South Africa: Please write to *Longman Penguin Southern Africa (Pty) Ltd, Private Bag X08, Bertsham 2013*

READ MORE IN PENGUIN

A CHOICE OF NON-FICTION

The Time Out Film Guide Edited by Tom Milne

The definitive, up-to-the-minute directory of over 9,500 films – world cinema from classics and silent epics to reissues and the latest releases – assessed by two decades of *Time Out* reviewers. 'In my opinion the best and most comprehensive' – Barry Norman

The Remarkable Expedition Olivia Manning

The events of an extraordinary attempt in 1887 to rescue Emin Pasha, Governor of Equatoria, are recounted here by the author of *The Balkan Trilogy* and *The Levant Trilogy* and vividly reveal unprecedented heights of magnificent folly in the perennial human search for glorious conquest.

Skulduggery Mark Shand

Mark Shand, his friend and business partner Harry Fane and world-famous but war-weary photographer Don McCullin wanted adventure. So, accompanied by a fat Batak guide, armed only with a first-aid kit and with T-shirts, beads and tobacco for trading, they plunged deep into the heart of Indonesian cannibal country . . .

Lenin's Tomb David Remnick

'This account by David Remnick, Moscow correspondent for the *Washington Post* from 1988 to 1992, of the last days of the Soviet Empire is one of the most vivid to date' – *Observer*

Roots Schmoots Howard Jacobson

'This is no exercise in sentimental journeys. Jacobson writes with a rare wit and the book sparkles with his gritty humour . . . he displays a deliciously caustic edge in his analysis of what is wrong, and right, with modern Jewry' – *Mail on Sunday*

READ MORE IN PENGUIN

A CHOICE OF NON-FICTION

The Time of My Life Denis Healey

'Denis Healey's memoirs have been rightly hailed for their intelligence, wit and charm ... *The Time of My Life* should be read, certainly for pleasure, but also for profit ... he bestrides the post war world, a Colossus of a kind' – *Independent*. 'No finer autobiography has been written by a British politician this century' – *Economist*

Far Flung Floyd Keith Floyd

Keith Floyd's latest culinary odyssey takes him to the far flung East and the exotic flavours of Malaysia, Hong Kong, Vietnam and Thailand. The irrepressible Floyd as usual spices his recipes with witty stories, wry observation and a generous pinch of gastronomic wisdom.

Genie Russ Rymer

In 1970 thirteen-year-old Genie emerged from a terrible captivity. Her entire childhood had been spent in one room, caged in a cot or strapped in a chair. Almost mute, without linguistic or social skills, Genie aroused enormous excitement among the scientists who took over her life. 'Moving and terrifying ... opens windows some might prefer kept shut on man's inhumanity' – Ruth Rendell

The Galapagos Affair John Treherne

Stories about Friedrich Ritter and Dore Strauch, settlers on the remote Galapagos island of Floreana, quickly captivated the world's press in the early thirties. Then death and disappearance took the rumours to fever pitch ... 'A tale of brilliant mystery' – Paul Theroux

1914 Lyn Macdonald

'Once again she has collected an extraordinary mass of original accounts, some by old soldiers, some in the form of diaries and journals, even by French civilians ... Lyn Macdonald's research has been vast, and in result is triumphant' – Raleigh Trevelyan in the *Tablet*. 'These poignant voices from the past conjure up a lost innocence as well as a lost generation' – *Mail on Sunday*

READ MORE IN PENGUIN

A CHOICE OF NON-FICTION

Stones of Empire Jan Morris

There is no corner of India that does not contain some relic of the British presence, whether it is as grand as a palace or as modest as a pillar box. Jan Morris's study of the buildings of British India is as entertaining and enlightening on the nature of imperialism as it is on architecture.

Bitter Fame Anne Stevenson

'A sobering and salutary attempt to estimate what Plath was, what she achieved and what it cost her . . . This is the only portrait which answers Ted Hughes's image of the poet as Ariel, not the ethereal bright pure roving sprite, but Ariel trapped in Prospero's pine and raging to be free' – *Sunday Telegraph*

Here We Go Harry Ritchie

From Fuengirola to Calahonda, *Here We Go* is an hilarious tour of the Costa del Sol . . . with a difference! 'Simmering with self-mocking humour, it offers a glorious celebration of the traditions of the English tourist, reveals a Spain that Pedro Almodovar couldn't have conjured up in his worst nightmare, and character-assassinates every snob and pseud' – *Time Out*

Children First Penelope Leach

Challenging the simplistic nostalgia of the 'family values' lobby, Leach argues that society today leaves little time for children and no easy way for adults – especially women – to be both solvent, self-respecting citizens and caring parents.

Young Men and Fire Norman Maclean

On 5 August 1949, a crew of fifteen airborne firefighters, the Smokejumpers, stepped into the sky above a remote forest fire in the Montana wilderness. Less than an hour after their jump, all but three were dead or fatally burned. From their tragedy, Norman Maclean builds an unforgettable story of courage, hope and redemption.